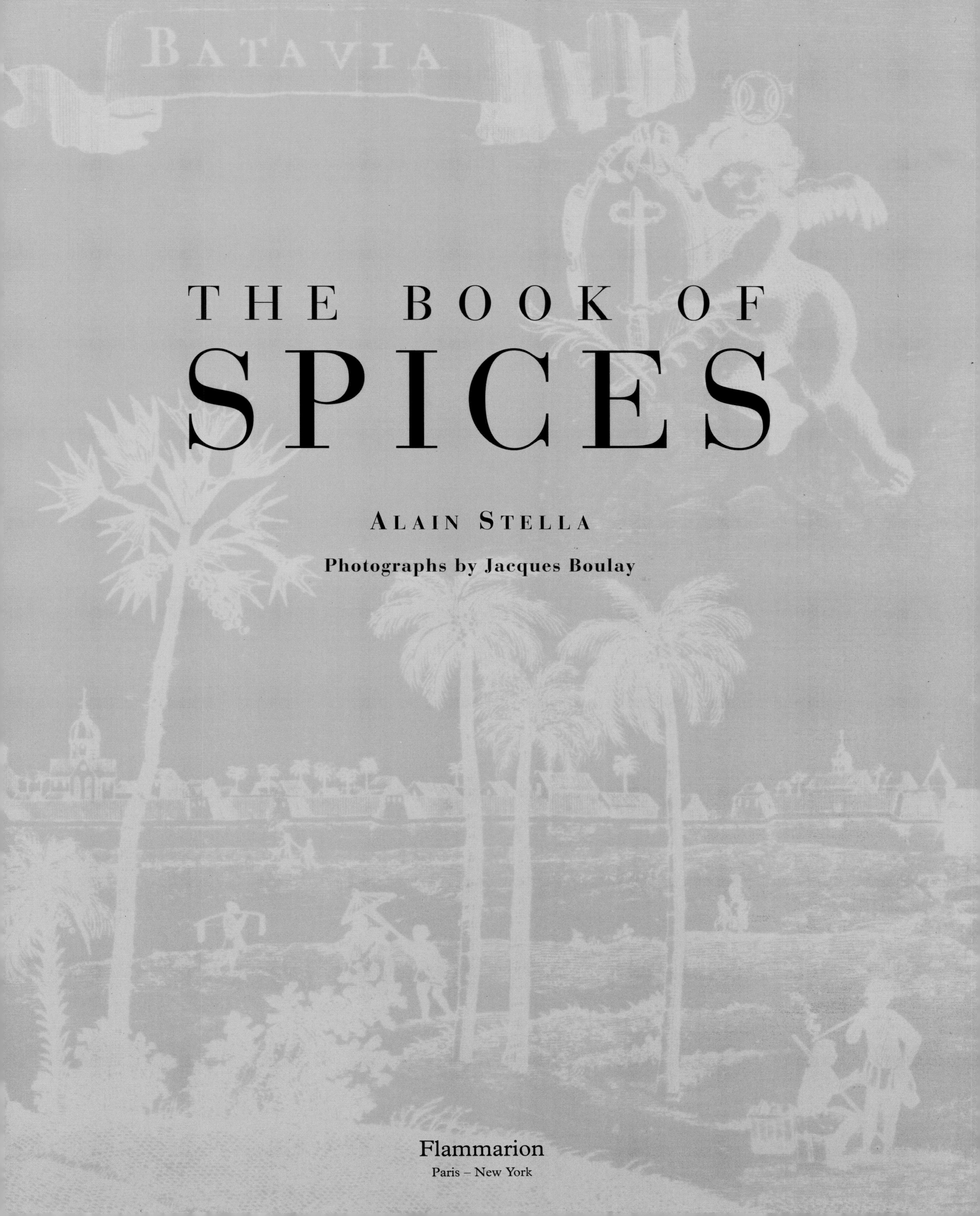

THE BOOK OF SPICES

ALAIN STELLA

Photographs by Jacques Boulay

Flammarion

Paris – New York

The bold adventurousness of the Frenchman Pierre Poivre (p. 7) who single-handedly managed to break the Dutch monopoly on nutmeg and clove in the eighteenth century is but one example of a life-long passion for spices. Today, chefs such as Olivier Rœllinger (p. 8 on a cardamom plantation in Kerala India) continue to search the world for the freshest ingredients to use in their recipes (p. 1, a blend of spices used for spice breads including cinnamon, clove, coriander and ginger ; p. 2, a Czech spice cupboard from the Paris spice shop Izraël; pp. 4-5, fresh vanilla pods; this page, a wooden box overflowing with saffron).

Designer
MARC WALTER/Bela Vista
Editor
GHISLAINE BAVOILLOT
Production Editor
Nathalie Bailleux
Production Manager
Murielle Vaux
Typesetting
Bela Vista
Photoengraving
Colourscan France

Original published in French under the title *Le Livre des Épices*
Copyright © 1998 Flammarion

Translated from the French by David Radzinowicz Howell and edited by Barbara Mellor

Flammarion
26, rue Racine
75006 Paris

Dépot légal: January 1999

ISBN: 2-08013-665-8
Numéro d'édition: FA 36657

Printed and bound in Italy by
G. Canale & Co. SpA, Borgaro

Contents

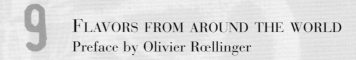

Flavors from around the World

by Olivier Rœllinger

In the beginning, there were the regions of France, each with their own way of cooking, their own produce, eating habits, rituals, and landscape. Then came the kings who united the provinces, and French cuisine made its entrance at court. A mirror held up to a period and to a kingdom, royal courts were receptive to fashion, to the arts and to those foreign influences on which the history of France is built. At the French courts one could hear echoes from the wars of the Holy Land, from the Italian Renaissance, of Dutch painting, of German philosophy, of Ottoman music and more. Great explorers-cum-merchants were then sent out by princes to ply the oceans, and new-found peoples learned of each other's existence. Routes to the West and East Indies were discovered, as were the sources of the Nile and the Yangtze, yellow gold and ebony wood; shady deals were brokered and friendships forged.

So it was that European ports, starting out as springboards to discovery, turned into soundingboards for countless far-flung cultures. And who were the people most receptive to these cultures? The ever-curious cooks who, in their thirst for knowledge, unearthed with each new discovery the novel flavor of a spice from a distant land. There gradually arose from the surprise—from the untold emotion that the awareness of the diversity of a people brings—a wholly new attitude, and a life-enhancing openness of spirit dawned. Beyond the talent and skill particular to each cook, it has been this awareness that has over the centuries raised French cuisine to an art form.

This dialog took more concrete form with spices. Spices provide a living reflection of our vision of the world as it concerns our relationships with other peoples.

During my childhood in Saint-Malo on the Brittany coast—the main port for the French South Sea Company even before it became the "Companie des Indes"— I would spend perhaps more time than other children with my eyes riveted on the open sea stretching beyond the city walls, daydreaming of improbable voyages and picturing in my mind's eye other shores under different suns. Over these childhood fantasies washed the scent of vanilla and cinnamon, nutmeg and benzoin, spices that were to become a rich treasure-house for an imagination enthralled by dreams of those extraordinary travelers from Brittany—seafarers, scientists, explorers, and writers such as Jacques Cartier, René Dugay-Trouin, Mahé de La Bourdonnais, Robert Surcouf, Jean Charcot and Chateaubriand. My chosen means of expression, cooking, has enabled me to convey the tradition and culture of this seaport whose story I tell through a vast range of spices which, just like a scented palette, has been widened by every far-flung or astonishing discovery. Today, the greatest European chefs are simply those who strive to take account of contemporary history by using different flavors from all over the world.

THE SPICE ROUTES

For thousands of years, spices have been providing us with the stuff of dreams, in addition to 'spicing up' our daily life. They transform the act of eating into both a pleasure and an art form, and are the source of the delicious flavor of all the exotic dishes—such as couscous, chili con carne, and curry—that are now common in our kitchens. They can miraculously enrich those all-too-plain meals that are often part of a low-fat diet. It is from them that not only the greatest head chefs, pastry-cooks, and chocolate-makers, but all cordon bleu cooks derive their inspiration, since spices give renewed vigor to one's creativity. But you do not have to don a chef's hat in order to grate a piece of ginger on a few lettuce leaves or sprinkle a pinch of cardamom on lamb, or paprika on some fresh goat's cheese, or pepper on strawberries. Spices have come to represent that extra touch of pleasure that our jaded palates—tired of everyday tastes—now crave.

In former times, when they were not so widely used and the prices they fetched meant that they were reserved for an elite, spices were the inspiration of countless dreams. In Antiquity, they served as a bridge to the gods. Without some mention of spices, it would be impossible to write a true history of religious belief. They provided too our very first medicines. Since the time of Alexander the Great, they have acted as a spur to the discovery and the exploration of new worlds. From the shores of Mexico to the coasts of India, following the monsoons perfumed with clove and nutmeg, the spice routes beckon us on an extraordinary voyage.

Luxuriant vegetation, unknown plants, indigenous peoples with surprising habits and customs, bizarre animals: this was how—fired by travelers' tales—the more or less imaginary paradisiac lands evoked by spices appeared to the eyes of astonished Europeans. Whether in the earliest pedagogical atlas (above, *Plants from India*, plate from an atlas showing the West and East Indies, printed in Leiden in the seventeenth century), or in painting (facing page, *The Nutmeg Harvest on the Island of Banda,* early nineteenth-century watercolor by Rudolph Verhull), the spice routes provided a means to dream. Preceding pages: the beautifully warm colors of a spice mix; stripping cinnamon bark in Ceylon in 1860.

SPICES IN ANTIQUITY

When did people first start adding spices to food? Probably during the Neolithic period, not long after pottery was invented. If the mastery of fire had long since meant that foodstuffs were no longer eaten raw, the emergence of the cooking-pot was to provide—thanks to a more subtle approach to cooking—the bases of a primeval gastronomy. At this point, our forebears began to crave still more intense tastes derived from the scents—be they flowers, trees, or grasses—that they encountered in the countryside and which proved a mysterious source of untold pleasure. When they were consumed, the body was filled with a soothing sense of well-being that perhaps also helped to alleviate pain. At the outset, then, spices offered human beings a dual benefit: one that was pleasurable yet physical. Surely the intangible and invisible magic of these blessings must derive from some supernatural power which should be venerated?

Pleasure, remedy, the sacred: this faith in the beneficent trinity that seemed to be combined in spices alone soon spread throughout the world. In the Euphrates and Nile valleys, archeological evidence points to the existence of a host of scents—and not only spices, but also incense and other fumigations— that were made as offerings to the gods in temples. On papyri, on the walls of tombs, the priests and kings of Egypt gave thanks for all the benefits dispensed by these "fragrances of the gods". Diffusing narcotic smoke from pistachio resin, from white incense or from myrrh that rose heavenward was an attempt to draw humanity closer to the divine, and no religious ceremony was complete without it. It was in the funerary ritual of embalming that aromatic substances were chiefly used, however.

"When they gather together to attend to a body," the Greek historian of the first-century BC Diodorus Siculus explained with reference to this process, "once it is opened, one of their number thrusts his hand into the corpse through a hole breached in the torso and extracts everything, leaving only the kidneys and the heart. Someone else cleanses all the entrails, washing them in palm wine and spices. The whole body is then treated painstakingly for thirty days, first with cedar oil and certain other preparations, and then with myrrh, cinnamon, and with spices that have the property of not only preserving the body for a long time but also endowing it with a most fragrant smell."

The aromas of spices, however, were not the exclusive privilege of the gods or of the dead. They also wafted through Egyptian kitchens, for we know that the Egyptians liked to cook their meat slowly with herbs and plants such as cumin, aniseed, fennel, coriander, and poppy seed. These local plants were not hard to find: their use was as often culinary, cosmetic or medicinal. This was far from the case with the aromatics that served as the basis for religious fumigations and ritual purifications, and perhaps for other more worldly pleasures in certain palaces belonging to the nobility or to pharaohs. The highly valuable trees that provided incense, bitter myrrh, fortifying cinnamon or other aromatic plants did not grow in the Nile valley and had to be imported from Punt, a country straddling the shores of the Red Sea. A number of archeological documents survive to bear witness to these trading expeditions, the most ancient inscription dating from 2300 BC, in the Fifth Dynasty. These were seafaring journeys, aboard long-hulled craft with both sails and oars, adorned on the prow with an ornament in the shape of a lotus flower. From Memphis or Thebes, they descended the Nile to the tip of the delta before entering its easternmost branch and making their way to the Red Sea through a series of canals and lakes. More adventurous maritime expeditions still, round the Arabian Peninsula

"All the birds of Punt swoop down to Egypt, spread with perfumes. The one that flies before takes my bait, exhaling the fragrance of Punt while his talons are coated with aromatic gum..." In Egypt, the most valuable spices and perfumes were brought over from Punt, a country that included both coasts of the Red Sea. Some spices, cinnamon for example, came from still more far-flung shores, from Asia, along the world's very earliest trade routes. In the temples of Egypt, aromatics and perfumed incense formed part of the offerings to the gods (facing page, pharaoh Tutmosis III offering up incense to the god Amon, from a bas-relief on Elephantine Island at Aswan.)

as far as the Euphrates–another region of incense and spices–are attested in the reigns of Tutmosis III and Ramses III.

To reach the Euphrates or Punt, these spices first had to come from a still more distant Orient. At that time, the different varieties of cinnamon–the first spice to appear in the texts–probably grew solely in India and China. Before the fourth century BC, scant material survives to enable an accurate reconstruction of the itinerary of these ancient routes which led from the Far East to the Mediterranean basin. Spices from the Indonesian archipelago were transported as far as India aboard junks. Cinnamon from Ceylon and China perhaps crossed paths with Indian pepper along the ancient caravan routes that traveled over the Afghan passes before continuing their way together on camelback across the Persian empire. Between India and Mesopotamia (today's Iraq), a large number of precious commodities must surely have been shipped down the coasts of the Persian Gulf.

Nonetheless, spices were to remain a mostly inaccessible luxury, as were myrrh and perfumed oils. Only members of aristocratic families were able to perfume themselves with cinnamon like the beautiful pupils of the poet Sappho. Poems by this "Tenth Muse", who lived in the seventh century BC, are the first writings in Greek to mention this spice, along with saffron. The Greeks were the first people to entertain a real passion for spices, the first to sacrifice whole fortunes in a quest for the pleasures offered by what were then exceptionally costly fragrances. For example, according to the spices and aromatics employed, a flask of perfumed oil might cost as much as one or even two slaves. Greek cooking too was seasoned primarily with a large number of Mediterranean potherbs, such as cumin, chervil, basil, savory and thyme, and, predictably enough, bay. Saffron, with its mauve flowers and precious carmine stigmas,

also grew in Greece. The flowers were used in the preparation of scented crowns and offerings to the gods in their temples; the stigmas were employed as a cloth dyestuff or, as it was believed to be an aphrodisiac, with cinnamon to flavor wine.

In the fourth century BC, Alexander the Great's conquests as far the banks of the Indus, as well as the maritime expeditions of his admiral Nearchos both there and to the mouth of the Euphrates, served to intensify East-West exchanges, and establish more plentiful and secure stopping places along the land routes and coastlines.

Two crucial events in trading history were to do much to foster the consumption of exotic spices on Mediterranean shores: the opening up two centuries later of a "Silk Route" between northeast China and Syria, and, not long afterwards, the discovery of the seafaring potential of the monsoon winds for navigation between India and the Red Sea. For two thousand years, until the arrival of steam ships, the alternating winds of the monsoon alone supported the extraordinary maritime activity between Asia and Africa, and, more specifically, the spice trade. If the geographer Strabo is to be believed, as early as 25 BC, "as many as one hundred and twenty craft" might be seen along coast of the Red Sea, "weighing anchor for the Indies". The monsoon winds that billowed their sails and swept across an almost uncharted ocean carried with them the scent of spices. On the return leg, holds were filled to the gunwales with cloves, ginger, cinnamon, cardamom, and above all pepper. Unloaded on the Egyptian coast, these spices proceeded to the Nile on the backs of camels before making their way to Alexandria by sail.

The Romans had a gastronomic passion for pepper. The great first-century Roman cook Apicius, who is considered to be the first true "chef" in history, used a great deal of pepper in all his recipes–some of which, such as boiled ostrich, stewed flamingo or stuffed sow's teats, seem somewhat flamboyant to our tastes. Festive dishes like these, as well as Apicius's recipes for sauces, contained cumin and at least half a dozen other aromatic ingredients, among them *garum*—a macerated fish sauce similar to the *nuoc-mam* of Vietnam—caraway, mint, honey, vinegar, wine, and coriander. It goes without saying that not every Roman was able to enjoy such lavishness, and in particular not the average citizen, for whom spices remained out of reach. At least they could breathe in the heady scents on their way around the Roman spice market, the *via piperatica*—or street of peppers—that showed off its exotic colors and fragrance from behind Trajan's forum.

Pepper, cloves, cinnamon, and cardamom all delighted the Roman palate. Pliny the Elder did not look kindly on the immense expense of this infatuation: "According to even the most conservative estimates," he scolded in his *Natural History*, "the Indies, China and the Arabian Peninsula exact one hundred million sesterces a year from our Empire." On the other hand, coriander, an aromatic plant growing near the Mediterranean coast, provided seeds that were both cheap and readily available (above). Their piquant, bitter, and fruity flavor was a favorite in Rome, where they appeared in recipes compiled by the cook Apicius, and they remain much in evidence in Eastern cookery.

"GINGER, PEPPER, CINNAMON AND OTHER SPICES..."

After the turbulent centuries that followed the fall of the Roman Empire, a fondness for spices re-emerged in the Middle Ages. The word itself appeared in English from the Old French (*espice*), and served to translate the Low Latin *species* that covered foodstuffs that were "special"–that is, rare or exotic. A passage from a thirteenth-century French medical treatise translated above evokes the properties of "*gyngembre, poivre, canele et autres espesses*". A well-known medieval romance that also became popular in England, *Le Roman de la Rose*, vaunted the benefits of the many "*espices délitables*" that were to be eaten after "rising from the table". The author specified "*après table*" since certain spices known as "confetti" or "chamber spices"–such as sugar-coated coriander seeds–were consumed after meals as an aid to digestion. Spices continued to be employed primarily in medicines and cookery. Belief in their medical powers knew no limits: during the great epidemics, spices and aromatic herbs were used in fumigations in the hope of purifying the pestilent air. It was in the use of kitchen spices, however, that the habits of medieval Europeans were to undergo a veritable revolution. Though the ingredients were available in markets at prices that restricted them to only the most lavish tables, cooking with spices, using every variety known today (with the exception of vanilla and the chili peppers that were only discovered later in the Americas), was raised to new heights by the virtuoso skill of the great chefs of the period. The most famous of them all, Guillaume de Tirel, known as Taillevent, was cook to Charles V. The collection of recipes that he composed around 1380, the *Viandier* (at the time, *viande*, which now only means "meat", denoted any foodstuff whether of animal or plant origin), provides magnificent testimony to the use of spices in the Middle Ages. This work was the inspiration behind the gastronomic section of the famous household guide *Le Ménagier de Paris*, compiled in 1393, a treatise intended for the management of borugeois homes.

"Pepper trees resemble vines," wrote the great fourteenth-century Moroccan traveler Ibn Battuta in his *Travels*. "They are planted close to coconut trees up which they climb... Pepper is picked in autumn and is laid out in the sun on matting, just as is done with grapes when they are dried." At much the same date, Marco Polo, in his *Divisament dou Monde* or *Travels,* was introducing western readers to the treasures of Asia (above, the pepper harvest). Another spice adored during the medieval period was saffron which was regarded as a fertility symbol: here it was used to give color and flavor to the risottos served in Bruegel the Elder's famous *Wedding Banquet.*

The most striking feature of such books is that spices are never absent from their pages. There is no dish that is not cooked in spices or else given added piquancy with some strongly flavored sauce. It has often been claimed that this plentiful and constant use of spices fulfilled the role of hygienically disinfecting foods and of masking their "spoiled" taste. This theory has been discredited, however, since we now know that the meats and fish consumed by the rich were for the most part fresh, and that the game was neither unhealthy nor repugnant. Above all, the concoctions dreamt up for these dishes were the result of much sophisticated research into particular flavors. Sauces that bind a spice to the acid juices of fruits, to verjuice or to vinegar bouillon—with breadcrumbs, starch or egg—gave the dishes a subtle bitter-sweet flavor that depended on both the basic food and the exact manner of cooking. Moreover, all these flavorings were obtained from a mixture of many spices, just as in the Orient today. "Cameline" sauce, for example, served with ox tongue and certain types of fish, combined ginger, cinnamon, cloves, "grains of paradise" (a kind of pepper to which we shall return later), mace (the outer shell of the nutmeg), and the longish fruit of a pepper called the *cubeb*. The proportion of each of these spices was not always precisely laid down, thereby leaving the exact dose to the flair and knack of the cook. Taillevent, however, prescribed a "ready-made" blend of powdered spices incorporating "four ounces of ginger, three and a half ounces of cinnamon,

two ounces of nutmeg, of cloves and "round" pepper [our normal peppercorn], one ounce and a half, of grains of paradise, and galingale, one ounce each." Quite properly, Taillevent recommended that the spices be added towards the end of cooking, "for the earlier they are put in, the more they lose their flavor". A princely table might thus boast mushrooms sautéed in spices, venison stew or a capon bouillon.

Pepper, the queen of spices since the time of ancient Rome, made an appearance in all these dishes. This commonest of all exotic spices was not particularly cheap, as testified by the old French saying, "as dear as pepper". Its value meant that it was often employed as a currency—for dues to the suzerain, for example, or as a dowry, or even as a fine imposed after some offense. Jews in the southern French town of Arles would pay the archbishop an indemnity of twenty pounds of pepper on Palm Sunday in exchange for his protection.

More generally, what were called "judges' spices" served to mollify or to thank a magistrate on the occasion of some court dispute. Such acts of bribery were to become commonplace and practically compulsory throughout the Ancien Régime; though it kept its old name, the gift of spices was gradually replaced with a contribution in cash. This was the payment "*en espesses*" that has left modern French with the expression "*en espèces*", meaning, "in cash". Originally, this payment would have been made in the form of the sort of expensive delicacies described above, in sugar drops or spice conserves.

In medieval kitchens throughout Europe, nutmeg and mace (the fibrous envelop that surrounds the nut's shell) were to meet with extraordinary success, especially in France, England, and Italy (above, an Italian painting of the late fourteenth century). In France, nutmeg proper–the "*nois mugades*" referred to in the *Roman de la Rose*–found its way grated into many a dish such as jugged hare, eel, and wild boar. In England, however, mace was preferred. Always scarce and expensive, spices could also serve as currency and were frequently used to pay off magistrates, lawyers or judges: spicy sugar-covered sweets were widely used as tender in law courts (facing page, *Peasant paying the Village Lawyer in Kind*, by Bruegel the Younger, 1621).

SINDBAD THE SAILOR AND THE MERCHANTS OF VENICE

Though the Arab invasion of Spain and the Crusades were to restore spices to the prestige they had enjoyed under the Romans, their countries of origin remained shrouded in mystery. Collective imagination filled gaps in knowledge with fabulous myths. In the narrative based on his travels, *Le Divisament dou Monde* (1298), even the Venetian merchant Marco Polo–who in the company of his father and uncle was one of the very few Europeans of the period to journey through Asia along the land and coastal routes–was to embellish accurate descriptions of things he had seen with amusing if tall tales purporting to give an account of distant lands teeming with cannibals and petrifying beasts.

The reason for this flight of fancy is simple: before the sixteenth century, apart from the Polos and a handful of Venetian or Genoese merchants, no European had ever ventured farther than the Asian coast of the Mediterranean. Beyond the great ports of Constantinople, Tyre and Alexandria, beyond the first stopping-places on the spice and silk routes such as Antioch, Aleppo or Palmyra, there lay a forbidden realm occupied by Persian, Arab, and Indian merchants. This trade network, bound together by a common faith, Islam, and a time-honored Arab merchant trading tradition (Muhammed himself was born of the tribe of the Quraysh who were merchants and caravan owners), extended throughout Asia to the great Chinese ports.

Sindbad the Sailor, a character out of the *Arabian Nights*, exemplifies perfectly the kind of fearlessness and business acumen typical of the Arab merchant. The numerous geographically accurate details in his tales make them seem authentic, and they are certainly based on the true adventures of ninth-century spice merchants. Sindbad's seven voyages carried him from Bagdad to India, to China and even it seems to Japan or Korea in his search for nutmeg, cloves, pepper, and ginger, as well as for pearls, precious woods, and camphor. Following his route, it is possible to draw a kind of map of the trade exchanges that ruled Asian seas over six or seven centuries. Starting out from the Arabian Gulf, Arab merchants arrived in Sri Lanka, India or Indonesia, where they purchased spices and other exotic produce, which they would then exchange in China against silk, lacquerwork, and porcelain. On the way back, they would once more take on supplies of spices and end up by making a fortune in Bagdad, Aleppo or Cairo. There, other middlemen would take on a share of the treasure and transport it to the shores of the Mediterranean.

It was on these shores that Venice awaited. The city-state had become a great power in the ninth century on the back of its formidable navy. In the fourteenth century, once it had sidelined its rivals Genoa and Pisa, Venice held what amounted to a monopoly over the European spice trade. In the shipyards of the Arsenale, more than a thousand shipwrights were hard at work building merchant and naval galleys. Twice a year, the city's Senate would decree the date on which the flotilla would weigh anchor for the Levant.

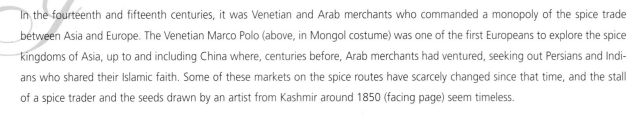

In the fourteenth and fifteenth centuries, it was Venetian and Arab merchants who commanded a monopoly of the spice trade between Asia and Europe. The Venetian Marco Polo (above, in Mongol costume) was one of the first Europeans to explore the spice kingdoms of Asia, up to and including China where, centuries before, Arab merchants had ventured, seeking out Persians and Indians who shared their Islamic faith. Some of these markets on the spice routes have scarcely changed since that time, and the stall of a spice trader and the seeds drawn by an artist from Kashmir around 1850 (facing page) seem timeless.

Escorted by an armada of galleys of the line, the convoy comprised a score of fine ships driven by forty or so oarsmen, whose task would sometimes be made less backbreaking by a good wind filling the sails. They would return a few months later–still in convoy in case of any unpleasant encounters–laden with spices, as well as with silks, cotton, and cereals. Their arrival back in Venice may easily be imagined: the crowds on the quayside, the sailors' homecoming, the unloading of the sacks whose scent filled the warehouses. Among all this merchandise was some that, once purchased by foreign traders, would be reloaded on to other galleys bound for France, Spain, Portugal or German lands. The fifteenth century saw the summit of the commercial power of Venice that provided an indispensable key for the trade in precious goods between Europe and Asia. The Republic had forged what appeared to be unbreakable links with the masters of Syria and Egypt, on whose shores these cargoes would arrive following their lengthy sea voyage. In exchange for spices and silks, the gold of Christendom flowed into the Serenissima's coffers.

Too long, however, did Venice slumber on those piles of gold, congratulating herself prematurely in the sumptuous Gothic palaces–such as the Ca' d'Oro and the Palazzo Dario–built on the proceeds. The centuries-old system that had made the Islamic powers of the East on the one side and Genoa and Venice on the other into the inescapable intermediaries between Europe and Asia was about to collapse, owing to the repercussions of the great voyages of discovery.

Towards the new spice lands

How could Venice have ever dreamed that the kingdom of Portugal, on an Atlantic coast then so far removed from the heart of the world, could, by disregarding the Levant altogether, dislodge her supremacy? Never could the Republic have imagined that, to reach the spice markets, there existed a route other than the Mediterranean ports, all of which lay under Venetian domination. With a false sense of security, Venice did not so much as bat an eye when Portugal, under the pretext of a crusade in 1415, seized Ceuta, a port on the African coast opposite Gibraltar which controlled the passage out into the Atlantic. But Ceuta was more than that: it represented the first step of the Portuguese into Africa, a continent whose riches could scarcely be guessed at, although it was already known as the source of Sudanese gold and a condiment from Guinea that resembled pepper, the fruit of the plant *Aframomum melegueta*. This spice came from a country so mysterious that it earned the

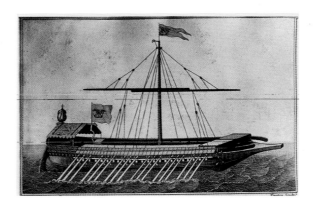

Venice's trade galleys, which formed the foundation of her power until the early sixteenth century, were designed to sail from the Serenissima to the Levant. They each shipped forty oarsmen and three hundred soldiers, among whom were numbered the much-feared crossbowmen in the prow, recruited from the minor aristocracy. Transporting the most valuable commodities, the finest being spices, they were regulated by a very exacting form of state control. Their speed, their security, and their independence with respect to the winds made them indomitable–at least on the Mediterranean.

name of "grains of paradise". Carried by camels to the shores of Tunisia or Tripolitania, and less costly though not as fine as Indian peppercorn, it had become a favorite in Europe during the thirteenth century. Ceuta was recaptured by the Moors in 1438, but not before one of King John I's sons, the Infante Henry, had set up another bridgehead to Africa, the port of Sagres on Cape Saint Vincent at the southernmost tip of the Portuguese coast, where he had taken up residence.

At Sagres, the prince whom they were to call Henry the Navigator had fitted out both a dockyard and a port from which he dispatched naval expeditions to the southern tip of Africa. In the course of a grandly ambitious mission, the Portuguese plundered Africa's wealth, its gold and all its various "grains of paradise"– and converted its inhabitants. As the seas were almost totally uncharted, this amounted to a complex project demanding thorough planning. In his library, the prince collected the works of all the learned geographers and travelers, a host of maps and globes, and gathered round him naval architects, mapmakers and astronomers, as well as the foremost mariners

By dint of carving out a new route to the Indies round the African coast and establishing itself in all the major ports of Asia as far as China, Portugal had become the uncontested master of the spice trade by the sixteenth century. The port of Lisbon (above, illustration by Théodore de Bry) was to become the crossroads for a commerce which extended into northern Europe. But the spice wars were only beginning. In the course of the following century, the Dutch took Ceylon and the Moluccas. The seizure of Kolang on the Malabar Coast in 1662 and the prosperous warehouses of Ambon in the Moluccas serve as magnificent backdrops for the Dutchman Johan Nieuhof's publication of 1682, *Les Voyages aux Indes Orientales* (following double page spread).

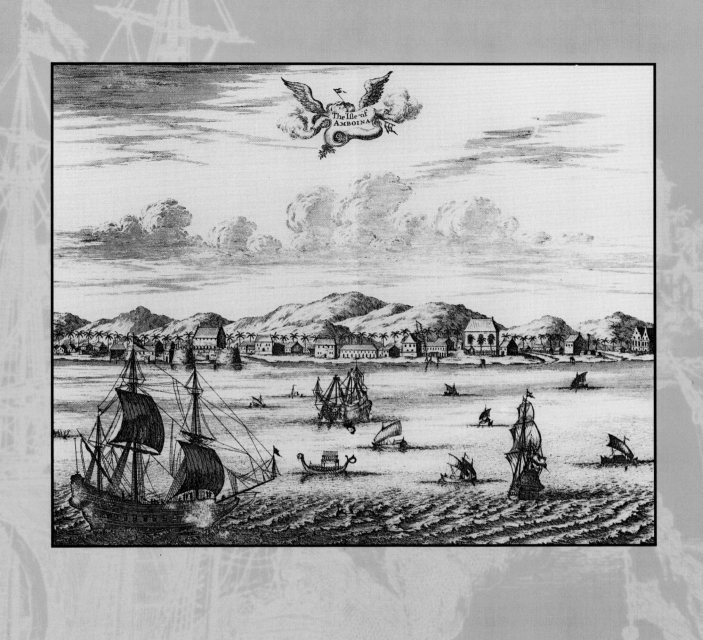

The Isle of
AMBOINA

from Genoa, Venice and the Arab lands. A number of sallies were organized, pushing ever farther southwards, each bringing back its own bounty of facts concerning winds, currents, and coastlines. The team in Sagres, after due examination, would pool this information to map out its famous pilot charts, the *portolanos*.

Henry died in 1460. For the sovereign who was crowned twenty years later, John II, the goal of navigation to the south lay not so much in the exploration of an essentially impoverished Africa but in the discovery of a new spice route to Asia. This maritime route would round the tip of Africa and thus dispense with the need for Venetian and Arab middlemen. In 1487 a violent squall pushed the three ships under captain Bartholomeu Dias out to open sea and around the Cape of Good Hope. The winds subsiding, the commander turned east, but finding no land there he then set off northwards, finally making landfall on the east coast of Africa on February 3, 1488. The new spice route was thus opened with, on the horizon, the Indian Ocean. Nine long years were to follow, however, before mariners ventured onto it.

Meanwhile, another route to the Indies was being carved out, to the west across the Atlantic Ocean. Nourished by the book of Marco Polo and imbued with his idea that eastern Asia, that is to say Japan, lay relatively near to Europe, the Genoese Christopher Colombus, after a fruitless attempt at the court of John II, eventually managed to convince the king of Spain, Ferdinand II. In 1492, he landed in the New World, certain that he thus had unveiled a new passage to Asia. From his first expedition, he

brought back neither gold nor spices, but instead a few "Indians". In the island of Hispaniola–later to become Haiti–however, Colombus's companions had spotted the presence of a spice as strong as pepper which they had christened with the name used for that plant in Spanish, *pimienta*: the pimento. This new spice was exported to Europe in any real sense only during the following century, at the same time as vanilla, newly discovered by Cortés among the Aztecs.

The somewhat disappointing results of Colombus's expeditions, and above all the treaty of Tordesillas of 1494 that laid down a line 370 nautical miles west of the Cape Verde Islands separating the parts of the world under Spanish dominion from those under the Portuguese, induced the latter to revert to an African route to the Indies. Captain Vasco da Gama and his four vessels cast off from Lisbon on July 8 1497. Their objective was the port of Calicut, the capital of the Malabar Coast, known as the Pepper Coast. After a series of misadventures on the east coast of Africa and crossing the Indian Ocean, Calicut was reached on May 20 1498. The city, governed by a Muslim rajah known as the *zamorin*, was then experiencing an extraordinary trading boom centered on the major commodities from India proper and the islands of the Indian Ocean: ginger, pepper, cinnamon, clove, and nutmeg, but also silks, lacquer, and porcelain, gem stones and exotic woods were loaded there on their way to Arab lands and Europe. Gama received a frosty reception from the *zamorin*, who had been forewarned of his approach by some Arab merchants and who recognized the

Vasco da Gama (above) required two military expeditions–in 1498 and 1502–to set up a Portuguese power base on the Indian coast of Malabar known as the Pepper Coast (facing page, on a seventeenth-century map). The second of these is particularly revealing of the methods employed at the time of the "spice rush". As a warning shot, a vessel carrying pilgrims on their way back from Mecca was taken some way off the Indian coast and set alight with all 380 passengers aboard. Arriving before the great spice port of Calicut, the Portuguese seized several Arab merchants on their boat, hanged them and cut them into pieces which they promptly sent to the Indian governor, who, petrified, hoisted the white flag and permitted them to anchor five of their warships.

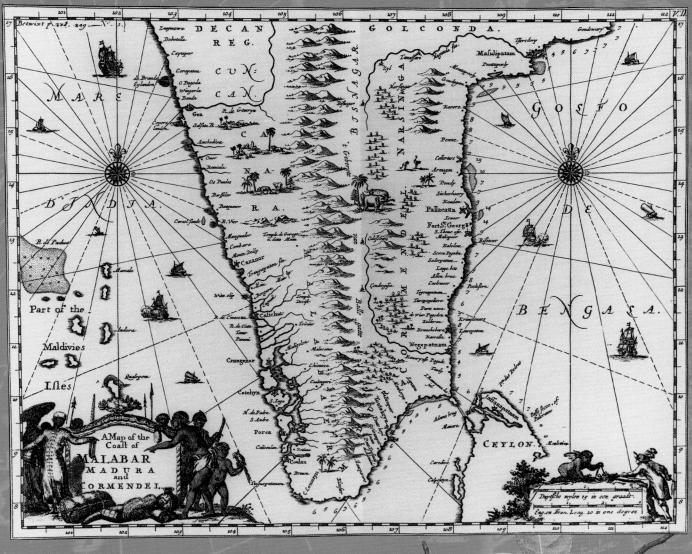

A Map of the Coast of
MALABAR
MADURA
and
CORMENDEL

danger that these newcomers represented. The voyage home was purgatory: two out of three men succumbed to scurvy and two ships had to be abandoned. But the holds of the remaining two overflowed with spices and precious stones, and Gama was received home in triumph. A new spice route had been forged.

This meant above all securing continued supplies and protecting them on the voyage, something only a military expedition seemed capable of accomplishing. There were a number of these, the one headed by Vasco da Gama returning to Calicut in 1502 with the intention of establishing a firm foothold there proving decisive. Gama was not content with Calicut, however, and continued skirmishing up the Pepper Coast, establishing the first Portuguese factory at Cochin. By 1503, the cost of pepper in Lisbon was a fifth of what it was in Venice.

THE ERA OF THE GREAT COMPANIES

This first spice war, which saw the Portuguese gain the upper hand in India, was to drag on nonetheless for a further ten years. In 1510, the Portuguese took the port of Goa and soon made it the capital of their colonial empire, the Estado do India. In 1511, it was the turn of Malacca, a port which controlled the entrance to the China Sea, then, in 1513, of Hormuz, thereby commanding the passage into the Persian Gulf. A few years later, the new king of Spain, Charles I (the future Emperor Charles V), seeing that the eastern spice route was henceforth shut to him, warmly received an offer from a Portuguese mariner who had fled Lisbon in disgrace, Fernão de Magalhães. Magellan, as he is known in English, proposed reaching the Moluccan archipelago, with its islands growing the most valuable spices such as clove and nutmeg, by sailing *westwards*. After amassing the necessary funds and having five vessels built, Magellan set sail on September 20 1519 from the Sanlùcar de Barrameda. The strait that was later to bear his name was discovered at the beginning of the subsequent year, followed by the Mariana Islands and by the Philippines in February 1521. It was there, on April 21, on a beach of the island Mactan, that the mariner

The steep and fertile peaks of the volcanic Moluccas Islands (above, Makyan, one of the islands of the archipelago, in a seventeenth-century Dutch print), the only place in the world where nutmeg and clove grow wild, were soon in the iron grip of the Dutch. The powerful East India Company in Holland (Vereenigde Oostindische Compagnie), which thus monopolized trade in the two most valuable spices, set up its headquarters (facing page) and its most important warehouses in Batavia, today's Jakarta (following double page spread, *Senior Merchant of the Dutch East India Company and his Wife before Batavia,* Albert Cuyp, c.1650). To protect this monopoly, any act of theft in its spice yards, guarded by halberdiers, carried the death penalty.

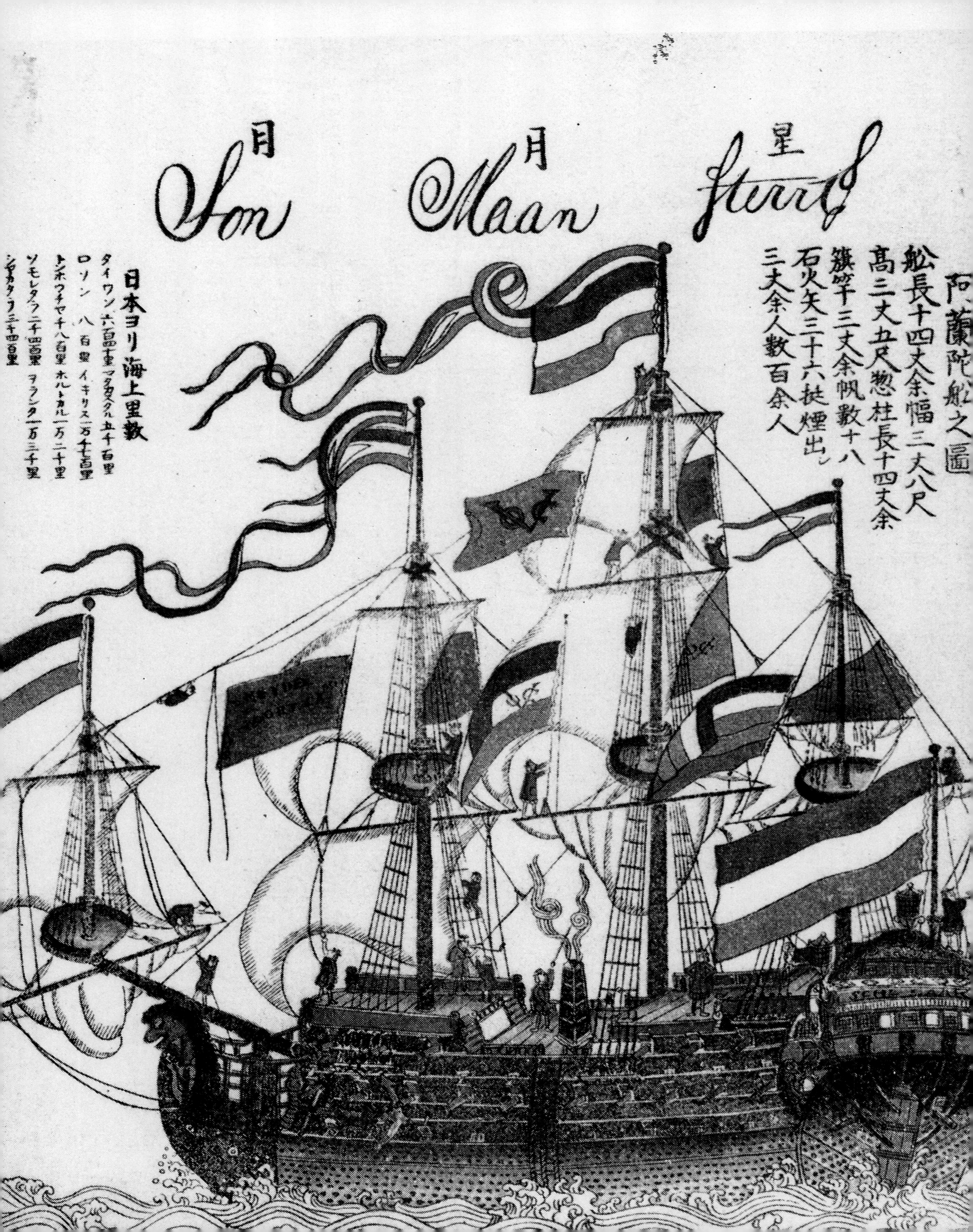

Son 月　　　Maan 月　　　Sterre 星

阿蘭陀船之圖

船長十四丈余幅三丈八尺
高三丈五尺惣柱長十四丈余
旗竿十三丈余帆數十八
石火矢三十六挺煙出ㇽ
三丈余人數百余人

日本ヨリ海上里數

タイワン六百四十里マタクル五千二百里
ロソン八百里イキリス二千七百里
トンキン千八百里ホルトカル一万二千里
ソモトラ二千四百里フランタ一万三千里
シヤム千三百四十里

was slain by aborigines. The expedition, although severely strained by a series of mutinies, continued its course, beaching at the Moluccas in November. The historian of the expedition, Antonio Pigafetta, tells how, in their flight from the Portuguese, the Spanish had just sufficient time to stuff the holds with nutmeg and clove, part of the spices being exchanged for "eighteen yards of rather fine red broadcloth". By going round the tip of Africa, and evading the eagle eye of the Portuguese, a single ship with eighteen survivors aboard arrived back in Spain on September 6 1522, thereby completing the first circumnavigation of the world.

Throughout the sixteenth century further expeditions designed to undermine the Portuguese monopoly were undertaken, this time by the French and the English along the spice routes. The most famous and ambitious of all was directed by an English privateer, Francis Drake. Setting off around the globe in 1577, following the same route as Magellan on the trail of Spanish galleons, he landed in the Moluccas. After sinking a Portuguese ship, he reached an agreement with the king of one of the isles richest in cloves, Ternate. The first Englishman in history to procure spices directly, he returned home to be received with the highest consideration by Queen Elizabeth. Once Portugal had been reunited with Spain in 1580, however, English dreams evaporated for the time being on the shores of Philip II's apparently invincible colonial empire. Yet even as this giant was girding its loins, Dutch Protestants, newly unified in their seven United Provinces under the banner of William of Orange, were throwing off the Spanish and Catholic yoke and proclaiming their independence. The war that followed and which dragged on until 1648 meant that, from 1594 onwards, Amsterdam shipping was forbidden roadsteads in any Portuguese or Spanish port. The fleet had for long been supplying all the Baltic ports with spices and other valuable commodities taken on at Lisbon, and had already acquired considerable muscle. It now saw itself cut off from its sources of supply. Well-organized and close-knit, disposing of vast capital resources, the Dutch merchants were not slow to react. Nine of them joined forces and founded a trading company, the Company of Distant Lands, with the intention to trade on the spice route themselves. The Company's inaugural expedition comprised four vessels laden with cloth and silver which left Amsterdam in the spring of 1595, reaching the island of Java after rounding the Cape of Good Hope and returning via the Moluccas. By the time they were welcomed home in triumph at the beginning of 1597, two-thirds of the crew had died of scurvy, and festivities were held in honor more of the regained independence of the Dutch people than of the half-filled bags of pepper and cloves that were unloaded from the hold. The two expeditions the Company financed the following year were far more profitable and encouraged the establishment of other similar enterprises. From their amalgamation in 1602 was born the Dutch East India Company, a joint-stock venture with a capital of six million florins. This was soon to become a powerful state within a state, a success in the Indies mirroring the decline of Philip II's empire.

"Of this day we have seventy men suffering from scurvy and bedridden. If we have to stay another week at sea, we will perish without fail. We have already thrown overboard one young man aged seventeen." This extract from *Le Voyage à l'Isle de France* by the author of the famous idyll, *Paul et Virginie*, Bernardin de Saint-Pierre, illustrates well the conditions aboard the vessels of the great trading companies (facing page, a ship of the Dutch East India Company). The voyage from Europe to Asia–usually without port of call–lasted between five and six months. Poor hygiene and scurvy took their toll among the crews (above, a dragoon in the French East India Company in 1791). The following double page spread: cinnamon, nutmeg and clove trees in the East Indies, from the *Leyden Atlas* (eighteenth century).

1. Arbre de canelle. 2. Comment on en tire l'écorce. 3. Lieu où on la Seche. 4. Noix Muscade. 5. Macis, ou
fleur de muscade. 6. Huile de muscade. 7. Muscadier. 8. Chasse des Elephans dans Ceylon.

1. Kaneel boom. 2. Kaneel schalling. 3. drooging. 4. Noot muscaet. 5. Folÿ. 6. Noot olÿ.
7. Noote boom. 8. d'Olÿfanten vangst op Ceÿlon.

KANEEL en NOOT

Canelle, Muscade, Chasse des Elephans, etc.

a Leide,

1. Clous de girofle . 2. Girofle . 3. Maniere donton recueille et seche les clous . 4. Bambou . 5. Canne .
6. Montagne qui vomit des flammes dans l'Ile de Ternate, une des Moluques .

1. Kruyt nagel . 2. Nagelboom . 3. Nagelvergadering en drooging . 4. Bamboes . 5. Rotting .
6. Brandende berg van Ternate .

KRUYT NAGELENGEWA

Girofle, Bambous,
Montagne brulante, etc.

Pierre van der Aa .

Too unwieldy and too scattered to be comfortably controlled, the Spanish empire, already undermined by piracy and lacking any real commercial direction, fell easy prey to the steely determination of the Netherlanders. Moreover, the Dutch, in contrast to the universal aspirations of the Spanish, focused from the outset on just one highly profitable commodity—spices—and thus on the single geographical area from which it came: India, its islands, and the Indonesian archipelago. What course of action, for example, lay open to the crew of the single Portuguese ship defending one of the richest spice islands of the Moluccas and Ambon, when in 1605, they were faced by a Dutch flotilla of fourteen vessels? Within half a century, the Dutch Company had acquired mastery of the spice islands. After the Moluccas, it was the profits accruing from Java, Malacca, Ceylon, Celebes and the Malabar coast of India to pour this time into Amsterdam's coffers. During these halcyon days of their colonial empire, only two other powers seemed capable of challenging the Dutch: the English East India Company, founded in London in 1600 under the gracious patronage of Queen Elizabeth I, and the French Compagnie des Indes Orientales, created by Louis XIV's all-powerful minister Colbert in 1664. Faced with Dutch superiority in the realm of spices, however, the former opted for trade with China in opium and tea, whereas the latter, from its trading-posts in Pondicherry and Chandernagore, preferred to turn its hand instead to cotton, silk, rice, and coffee. So it was that the Dutch—all the more so after wresting Ceylon and its cinnamon from the Portuguese in 1604—reigned supreme throughout the seventeenth century. In Batavia (today's Jakarta) the flourishing capital of their East Indian empire founded in 1619, merchants and administrators rode in gilded coaches. From all the islands of the Indian Ocean, spices flowed into Batavia, where they were stored prior to making their way to Europe in armed convoys.

As early as the end of the sixteenth century, galvanized by the buccaneering exploits of Sir Francis Drake, the English had begun to dream of building up a colonial empire of their own in the Indies. Created in 1600, the East India Company established its first trading-post in India in 1611, but it faced stern opposition from Dutch pre-eminence in the spice trade, and it was only at the end of the eighteenth century that it gained the upper hand in India and Ceylon. As a result, the London docks and the quarters of the city involved in the trade with the East Indies were then to experience a period of intense activity (above, *View of the East India Docks*, watercolor by William Danielli, 1908; facing page, *Leadenhall Street*, watercolor by Thomas Halton, 1800).

Although the main actors in the pepper and cinnamon trade were the Dutch, they derived their dominant position essentially from the two most coveted spices—nutmeg and clove—that grew in the Moluccas and nowhere else. Naturally, this was a characteristic which signally favored the Dutch, since the control of a single archipelago proved sufficient to ensure a global monopoly. At the outset, however, the surveillance of this valuable archipelago, with its three larger islands and an infinity of smaller islets scattered over a sea covering an area ten times that of the Netherlands, presented insurmountable difficulties. Its far-sighted new masters concentrated the entire production on to a small number of tiny islands—nutmeg on the Banda Islands, cloves on Ambon—and destroyed all the spice trees growing elsewhere. Henceforth, any unauthorized plantation, or even the theft of a single shoot, was punishable by death. With the territory under firm control, it remained only for the Dutch to ensure a high price for their spices thanks to a policy of limited supply on production. Better than expected harvests could be stockpiled for years in warehouses, or else, in the course of spectacular festivities, mountains of surplus spices could simply go up in smoke. The great and the good of Batavian society would be invited to a banquet held in front of a vast esplanade on which a bonfire was lit. Great piles of nutmeg and clove would be kept burning throughout the night, releasing an exquisite perfume that was both deliciously pleasurable to the dancers and singularly profitable for the traders.

"Do you like nutmeg? We've put it everywhere…" These ironic lines by the seventeenth-century poet Boileau are revelatory of the value that had been ascribed since the Middle Ages to this "rare spice plant", one of the costliest commodities in the world, which for many years grew solely in its native haunt of the Moluccas. For centuries, it was prized by the inhabitants of India, Arabia and China for its virtues both culinary and medicinal, while the great nations of Europe were to fight over it with fire and cannon. The Dutch restricted production to the easily monitored Banda Islands, but by the eighteenth century their monopoly had been broken. Thanks to the English, the attractive flower of the nutmeg tree (above)—harbinger of its delicious fruit—could soon be seen blooming on Ceylon (facing page, a plantation around 1850), in Malaysia, on Singapore and on Grenada.

THE ADVENTURES OF MONSIEUR POIVRE

For more than a century, no great maritime company, no fleet of men-of-war ever succeeded in breaking the Low Countries' monopoly on the most costly spices. One man alone–an obstinate Frenchman named, by a strange quirk of fate, Pierre Poivre (that is, "Peter Pepper"!)–managed to purloin this treasure from the Dutch and offer his native land the chance of cultivating its own spices.

It was in Batavia in 1745 that this dream took shape in the brain of the young Pierre Poivre. Then aged twenty-six, Poivre, the son of a mercer from Lyon, had already undergone his fair share of adventures. Four years earlier, as a novice on a foreign evangelical mission he had been sent to China and then on to Cochin China. Dismissed from the congregation in 1744, he embarked for Canton in order to make his way back to France on the *Dauphin*, a vessel belonging to the Compagnie des Indes laden with Chinese silks. In February 1745, passing through the narrow strait of Bangka that lies between the island of the same name and Sumatra, the *Dauphin* was attacked by an English flotilla of frigates and brigs: not only in Europe but in the South Seas too, the War of Austrian Succession opposed the French and the English. During the skirmish, Pierre Poivre lost his right arm, torn off by a cannon ball. The French were taken prisoner and dragged off to Batavia where the English released them. The *Dauphin* and its cargo was sold off.

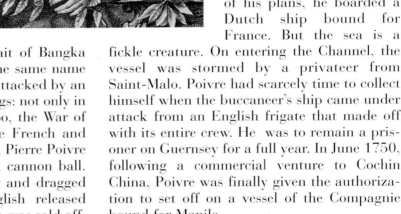

Poivre stayed in Batavia for four months, time enough for his amputated arm to heal. During this stay in the opulent capital of the Dutch East Indies, Poivre would pace up and down along the port in front of warehouses drenched in the scent of cloves and contemplate the spices being loaded onto the magnificent ships of the Amsterdam Company. To ensure its monopoly, guards were posted everywhere: not a single seed could go astray. It was there that the idea of making off with part of this treasure slowly dawned on the young man. All he needed was a few grains of nutmeg and clove plant that he could then try to grow on land in the Indies belonging to the French.

The following year, we catch up with Poivre in Pondicherry, where he met Mahé de La Bourdonnais, governor of Île de France and Île de Bourbon (later to become Mauritius and Réunion). Poivre followed the great mariner back to Île de France where he encountered a soil well suited to spice-growing. Keen to persuade a minister or two at Versailles of the good sense of his plans, he boarded a Dutch ship bound for France. But the sea is a fickle creature. On entering the Channel, the vessel was stormed by a privateer from Saint-Malo. Poivre had scarcely time to collect himself when the buccaneer's ship came under attack from an English frigate that made off with its entire crew. He was to remain a prisoner on Guernsey for a full year. In June 1750, following a commercial venture to Cochin China, Poivre was finally given the authorization to set off on a vessel of the Compagnie bound for Manila.

Like its sister plant, nutmeg, the extremely fragrant Molucca clove, whose very leaves give off a scent on the tree (facing page, a clove tree), which in the past excited a considerable degree of covetousness. Known for three thousand years in India and China, its European market was cornered first by the Portuguese and then by the Dutch before, in 1770, an expedition organized by Pierre Poivre (above) managed to appropriate a few dozen stocks from the tiny island of Batavia. Henceforth, the clove was to thrive in the French colonies. From the nineteenth century onwards, under the impetus of Sultan Said, the island of Zanzibar was to become the world's foremost producer; by 1895, one hundred and forty thousand African slaves worked on the clove plantations there.

Poivre remained several months in Manila, gleaning information on the Moluccas from the seamen from all four corners of the earth who would stop off in the Philippines. He thus came to learn that a few of the archipelago's smaller islets growing cloves and nutmeg were not closely guarded by the Dutch. Miraculously, he even managed to acquire in Manila a few mace plants and nuts capable of germination. Packed off to the Île de France, they were later to perish through neglect. Poivre himself returned to the island with more nutmeg seeds, thereby proving that the Dutch monopoly could indeed be broken, but sadly they were too few in number for cultivation to be possible. Before setting out once more to the Indies, he entrusted them to the curator of the island's botanic gardens, the "Réduit", where they survived all too briefly. It later transpired that the curator, envious of Poivre's success, had destroyed them deliberately. A few more plants wild nutmeg, brought back from Timor in June 1755, were once more sabotaged by the official botanist on Île de France.

At his wit's end, Poivre then made up his mind to return to mainland France. He acquired a property near Lyon where he remained for ten years, composing a multitude of scientific reports. One of these, inspired by the spirit of the Enlightenment and devoted to the customs of the "peoples of Africa and Asia", was printed by an Amsterdam printer under the title *Voyages d'un philosophe*. The work was appreciatively read in high places, and, in 1766, the Duc de Choiseul summoned Poivre to Paris and offered him the post of Intendant—or governor—of Île de France. Poivre duly accepted. Under the direction of its new Intendant, the island soon put its finances on a firm footing which renewed its agricultural development. Poivre set an example by purchasing a property named "Mon Plaisir", to become known as the "Grapefruit Garden". Poivre turned this into an extraordinary botanic and zoological garden with all that was most exotic from those parts of the French empire, and gradually grew there every kind of plant from the Indian Ocean.

Sorely taxed by his governmental and agricultural work, Poivre could no longer dream of going off himself on a hunt for the nutmeg or clove. In the spring of 1768, therefore, he charged the captain of a ship, *L'Utile* with just such a mission. This first expedition ended in disaster: when storms, misadventures at the hands of a petty ruler of Timor, scurvy, and other tropical illnesses had taken their toll, only a single crewman survived to tell the tale. The following spring, a second expedition with two vessels, the *Vigilant* and the *Étoile du matin*, set out. After several months at sea, the two ships went their separate ways: the *Vigilant* headed for Timor from where, fifteen years earlier, Poivre had brought back some nutmeg, while the *Étoile du matin* made for the Moluccas. The former returned empty-handed, but the latter was to earn its place in the history of spices. Slipping past the Dutch fleet and garnering information from island to island before joining forces with several local chieftains, the *Étoile* and its men reached the small island of Batanta where they were received as liberators by the population. The island was overgrown with wild nutmeg and clove plants. In June 1770, the *Étoile* was at last able to unload its cargo on to the quayside of Port-Louis on Île de France, before being immediately sent on to "Mon Plaisir": it contained several hundred stocks of nutmeg and clove as well as thousands of nuts and grains. The Dutch monopoly was broken. A year later, Poivre was elevated to the status of nobility and the brand new "Chevalier Le Poivre" was appointed Commissioner General of the Navy. Nutmeg and clove were expedited to Île Bourbon, to Madagascar and to Guyana for cultivation. In the "Grapefruit Garden», the first clove fruits saw the light of day in 1775, while the first harvest worthy of the

In 1930, under the watchful eye of a Dutch colonial overseer, the nutmeg pickers of the small islands of Banda in the Moluccas hand over their crop (facing page, above). To gather in the harvest, they are equipped with a *gai gai*, the long bamboo-cane pole still in use today. The kernel and the fine red mace will be extracted from the fruit; the kernel is split open to reveal the seed, the "nut" of nutmeg. Following double-page spread: a southern French port which owed its prosperity to the spice trade, Toulon (*A View of the Old Port* by Joseph Vernet).

name was taken in two years later, with nutmeg following shortly afterwards. Already back in France by 1773 having sold his estate to the king, Poivre ascended to the eternal spice lands in 1786.

SPICE MERCHANTS OF TODAY

A quarter of a century after the death of Pierre Poivre, the English seized Mauritius and his "Grapefruit Garden" for themselves and so "French" clove and nutmeg trees were packed off to bloom on Madagascar, the Comoros and in the West Indies. On the newly redrawn map of the world's exotic flavors, spices had become less important as goods for trade. Traders—and with them the pioneers of the food industry—were now making their fortune with sugar, cacao or tea as much as with cinnamon or ginger. As early as the sixteenth century, the extravagant consumption of spices had been succeeded by a more moderate, more thoughtful use that took increasing account of the original flavor of the foods. At the same time, national preferences for certain spices were taking shape: French cooking opting for the flavor of nutmeg, English for mace and Spanish for saffron. And, as the century advanced, so spices slowly disappeared from cook books. Now that they were less scarce and more widespread than before, some writers had begun to find them commonplace. The way they forced themselves on the taste buds, thrusting aside

every other flavor, smacked of boorishness. In his *Repas ridicule* of 1665, the court poet Boileau poured mockery on a table that flaunted an inferior, bourgeois sense of taste: "Do you like nutmeg?/ We've put it everywhere./ Ah! Messieurs, these chickens taste superb!" The fashion had played itself out. The best society now preferred sweet sugar, sensuously dizzying chocolate and intellectually stimulating coffee. This waning in popularity lasted well into the twentieth century.

From Dumas' *Grand Dictionnaire de Cuisine* to Marie-Antoine Carême and Brillat-Savarin, the great treatises of gastronomy cease to mention spices. It should be noted that this rejection was less pronounced in England, even at the court of George IV, in whose service Carême was a cook. He reports how his royal master, when still Prince Regent, demanded such a quantity of spicy dishes that he "often suffered pains throughout the day and at night".

If spices were no longer to be found on such princely tables, they continued to waft through the dispensaries of "peppermen" and apothecaries, where the middle classes purchased their provisions. In the eighteenth and nineteenth centuries, as a bourgeoisie emerged that hankered after a better quality of life—especially as to the pleasures of the table—a number of these "engrossers" were to make their fortune. William Fortnum and Hugh Mason, who founded in 1707 the celebrated London store that still bears their names , were the forerunners of the great grocery dynasties that were to service the needs the urban elite. Before joining forces

Long available solely through small-scale spice sellers and apothecaries, spices were to become available to a new market at the end of the nineteenth century thanks to the creation of the very first "supermarkets" specializing in foodstuffs. In the warehouses of all the major western ports, wholesalers would purchase spices from every continent at auction (above, nutmeg and mace being sold at a sale in Amsterdam; facing page insert, cinnamon being inspected before auction in London). Cinnamon (facing page)—"child of a distant soil that makes one forget the rose's scent", as Petronius wrote long ago—remains one of the most sought-after spices.

with his landlord Hugh Mason, William Fortnum, footman at the Court of Queen Anne, had already had some success trading in the leftover candles that were replaced every day in the chandeliers in the palace.

It took fully two generations for this little business to transform itself into a luxury grocery store, by which time the founders' heirs had become suppliers to the Court in candles, and, above all, in edibles such as tea, fine wines and spices. By the end of the eighteenth century, the house of Fortnum & Mason was the main purveyor of spices in London, kept amply supplied by a few Fortnum cousins who had joined the East India Company. Also in London, Harrods, whose celebrated Food Hall teems with customers today, opened in 1849. In 1743, in Amsterdam, it had been the turn of the druggist-cum-herbalist, Jacob Hooy, whose magnificent shop still stands on the Kloveniersburgwal. In Paris, Ferdinand Hédiard, sensing the arrival of a fondness for things colonial that was to culminate in the great International Exhibitions, inaugurated his store known as the "Comptoir d'Épices et des

Colonies" in 1850. There too in 1886, Auguste Fauchon, after an apprenticeship spent under the eminent grocer Félix Potin, opened the fine food store filled with exotic produce that remains to this day on Place de la Madeleine. The undiminished curiosity of city-dwellers for exotic cuisine could thus be satisfied, while in London, Amsterdam, Antwerp, Philadelphia, and Chicago, the great Universal Exhibitions of the end of the century presented enthusiastic crowds with ever more novel experiences for the taste buds. At the 1900 Exposition Universelle in Paris, visitors could visit two Indian restaurants—one situated in the French pavilion for the Indies, the other in that belonging to the English colonies—several "exotic restaurants" in the Algerian pavilion, an "authentic restaurant of the Celestial Empire" in the Chinese, and "Turkish and Arab restaurants" in the Turkish. Only in the course of the following century, however, by which time industrialists had taken up the running, can it be said that the general public's renewed infatuation with spices had well and truly taken root. Between the wars, companies

*I*n addition to the exoticism of spices, their captivating aroma, superb coloring, smooth feel, and exquisite flavor, which since the beginning of the twentieth century have finally become accessible to all, make them an eternally magical commodity. Wholesale and retail grocers vie with each other in creativity (left, spiced oil perfumed with cinnamon, green cardamom, mace, cumin, clove makes an aromatic salad dressing), but also in the care and safeguards required (right, selecting and treating mace in Amsterdam, 1925) in order to present their customers with ever more alluring produce. Packaging, meanwhile, could be transformed into a casket for the most precious condiments, such as this exceptionally fine turn-of-the-century box for vanilla sticks (facing page).

such as McCormick in the United States (today the biggest retailer in the world), Daamhouver in the Netherlands, and Noel's in Great Britain restored spices to their former popularity. See-through bottles and small sachets replaced sale-by-weight making both distribution and conservation less problematic.

In France, the since defunct firm of Aussage launched the famous little cardboard serving sachet, triangular in section, for pepper: a minor revolution still remembered by many grandparents. Pre-packaged–and even deep-frozen in the case of unripe green pepper and "pink peppercorn"–spices have made inroads into every kitchen. The ebb and flow of migrations, "globalization", and the democratization of tourism mean that no large city is without its "exotic" delicatessen and restaurant, and that no bookstore is with-out books on West Indian, Moroccan, Indian or Chinese cooking. But spices are not now consumed solely in dishes from exotic climes: harking back to the breadth of vision possessed by the cooks of yesteryear–and yet mastering the delicate alchemy of their aromas better than their forebears–a number of chefs are today creating a sublime cuisine. Here, it is local produce and ancestral traditions that are given a new lease of life thanks to the flavors of distant lands. The "young lobster with spices" that Oliver Roellinger serves in his restaurant at Cancale on the Bay of Saint-Malo is a splendid example of this "comeback" staged by the spices of the Middle Ages, India and Grenada caressing the shellfish meat like some scented wind from a tropical current, blended with the sea air, iodine, and spray of the Breton coast.

In 1874, in his fashion review, *La Dernière Mode*, the symbolist poet Stéphane Mallarmé, before going on to quote a recipe for chicken curry with coconut milk that he had been given by a storekeeper on the Boulevard Haussmann, noted a desire of French cooks "to acclimatize us to products and preparations from all over the world".

The first of the fine food stores in Paris to respond to this desire was the "Comptoir des Épices et des Colonies" founded by Ferdinand Hédiard in 1850 on Rue Notre-Dame-de-Lorette (above). The shop took its present name when it moved to the Place de la Madeleine four years later, where still today it presents a magnificent array of spices (above, insert). Facing page, the grocery store Félix Potin, another temple to fine eating, in the 1920s.

Around 1920 in France, Maurice Marchand of the firm of Aussage created his little triangular box inspired by Toblerone chocolate that was soon after to be equipped with a pourer (above, a range of spices from Aussage organized by Pierre Marzorati at the historical grocery museum, the Musée de l'Épicerie d'autrefois, at Lignerolles in the departement of Orne). In the United States, the firms of McNess and McCormick (above) also offer their products in packaging designed to be easy to use and ensure good conservation. Vying with the industrial giants, prestigious spice stores offer their customers incomparably fresh spices sold loose. Two examples are the firm of Jacob Hoy founded more than two centuries ago in Amsterdam (facing page), and the overflowing stock at the Maison Izraël in Paris (following double page spread).

Thanks to her outstanding vineyard at Château de la Tuilerie, near Nîmes in the south of France, Chantal Comte has breathed new life into the spice wines of antiquity with her refreshing "Elixirs": "Carthagène" (facing page) with natural spices should be drunk as an aperitif or with dessert; the white goes well with foie gras or Roquefort cheese. The irresistible fruit delicacies made by Christine Ferber (above) have deliciously transformed traditional condiment- and preserve-making. From top to bottom: candied rhubarb with Gewürztraminer and pepper, for salmon or Roquefort; candied quince with orange and spices for game; Williams pear conserve with vanilla; damson conserve with cinnamon; quince conserve with "Nostradamus's spices" (cinnamon, cardamom, cloves, and star anise).

THE SOVEREIGN SPICES

Of the hundred or so spices that caress—or inflame—our palates, barely a dozen merit the title of "sovereign": unlike the others, which remain the preserve of a handful of chefs, these have made their mark in kitchens all over the world. From cinnamon to vanilla, from clove to capsicum, they are adored by people from every continent. Flowers or seeds, bark or fruit, rhizome or nut, they may be sweet or spicy, subtly bitter or divinely suave. They may hail from India or Granada, China or Guinea, Turkey or France. The name of "spice" that they share indicates their exceptional flavor and their vegetable origin, but above all the sensuousness of their world and that uncanny ability they have of surprising us—and of inspiring us to dream. Without spices our cooking would be bland; and without spice our lives would soon descend into boredom. Before looking at the spices that have conquered the world and the mixes that can blend them into novel flavors, we should remember that every one of these treasures must be looked after with the greatest care: stored in an airtight container, they should be ground, crushed, and prepared at the last minute in order to be enjoyed in their full splendor.

Initially, spices seduce with the magic of their color and their perfume. In the souks of the Orient (above, in Morocco), sightseers and spice lovers alike can experience these sensual delights with rare intensity and heightened anticipation. Nonetheless, spice flavors are best captured when they are conserved away from air and dust. This is what the very best stores selling spices offer their customers today. Only recently in London, Terence Conran created just such a shop, a gastronomic temple known as "The Bluebird Store", where fresh spices are carefully packaged in small, hermetically-sealed tins (facing page). Following pages: an array of fine spices for aromatic cooking. Preceding pages: small spice bags and fresh vanilla from Madagascar.

BLUEBIRD
Ground Cloves

Best Before End 1999.

Bluebird Store Ltd 350 King's Road London SW3 5UU

58g

BLUEBIRD
Tandoori Curry
Powder

Coriander, Cumin, Salt, Paprika,
Cinnamon, Cloves, Colouring

King's Road London SW3 5UU

66g

Cinnamon,
bark of paradise

Cinnamon—of mysterious and ancient origin—has been perfuming the Mediterranean coast for three or four thousand years. Even before the spice cast its spell over our taste buds, the exquisitely deep yet mild spiciness of its scent evoked images of paradise for the Ancients. Describing the body of his beloved, Solomon in the *Song of Songs* evokes the marvelous garden in which cinnamon was born, through which drift scents of "spikenard and saffron; calamus and cinnamon".

A FABLED AROMA

From the Mediterranean to China, every ancient civilization knew and adored the bark of the attractive tree that we know as cinnamon. Strictly speaking, we should refer to cinnamons in the plural, since at the time a distinction had already been made between Chinese cassia (*Cinnamonum obtusifolium*, var. *cassia*, known to the Greeks as *kasia*) and cinnamon from Ceylon, less coarse and more fragrant, which the Greeks called *kinnamon* (*Cinnamonum zeylanicum*). Rare in Egypt prior to the Ptolomaic period, cinnamon was nonetheless occasionally employed in embalming, and was offered up to the gods in fumigations. Its origins were to remain cloaked in mystery until the Middle Ages. In the fifth century BC, Herodotus alleged that it could be found in Arabia, more precisely in a lake inhabited by "beasts endowed with wings very similar to our own bats that possess a terrifying scream and are immensely strong: when collecting the cinnamon, one has to protect one's eyes from attack". Only the spice merchants themselves knew perhaps that the smooth bark, transported by Arab mariners and then by the caravans of the desert, in fact came from far-off Asia. The warming and slightly peppery aroma of Ceylonese cinnamon was a delight to the cooks of the medieval period. On their return from the Crusades, "goodly knyghts" brought it back in their bags, handing it to their pages to be used in the preparation of an invigorating wine. This delicious cordial, that Rabelais was later to celebrate under the name of *hypocras*, also contained cloves. Medieval gastronomy, above all, was impregnated with the scent of cinnamon. It was much venerated in France where it was used in two-thirds of the dishes and sauces prepared by the country's master cooks. Following the discovery of the New World with its cacao and vanilla, the Spanish of both the mainland and the colonies took delight in a half-American, half-Asian chocolate drink, fragrant with the aromas of cinnamon, vanilla, and anise. Enthusiasts for the drink soon sprung up all over a Europe that was kept plentifully supplied with cinnamon by merchants from Venice.

THE CINNAMON GARDENS

Today, as in the past, the best cinnamon bark in the world continues to come from Sri Lanka. Between the monsoons, this splendid island, so rich in artistic traditions and in the scents of flowers, spices, and tea, is caressed by a heavenly breeze which blows through the cinnamon gardens concentrated in the southern portion of the island, on the sunny lowlands around Galle and Colombo. During the rainy season, between May and October, cinnamon-strippers, naked to the waist wearing a loincloth of Madras and armed with a hatchet,

Cinnamon (facing page) has been providing its soft and tender bark since Antiquity. The Romans considered it a panacea, able to warm the body, ease digestion, and treat eye troubles as well as snake bites. Its stimulant properties were well known in India. In a fine novel recently published in London, *The Mistress of Spices,* Chitra Banerjee Divakaruni describes it as a "destroyer of enemies to give you strength, strength which grows in your legs and arms and mostly mouth till one day you shout *no* loud enough to make them, shocked, stop". Its qualities were also appreciated by students at Oxford, who used to serve elegantly prepared slices of buttered toast sprinkled with cinnamon.

can be seen bent over between rows of large shrubs with deep green leaves. Since it has been grown and cultivated, cinnamon has been kept as a shrub no more than six feet high. Before cutting its numerous branches, cultivators wait for the rainy season and the appearance of the new leaves, for this is the moment when the rising sap makes it easier to peel off the bark and the most intense aromatic compounds are fixed. Sometimes they can be seen carrying over their shoulder bundles of long, thin branches less than an inch in diameter, whose color is already evocative of cinnamon as we know it; these are then taken to shelters—often no more than large huts of woven palm leaves—to await their metamorphosis.

Watching the work that takes place here amounts to an experience in time travel: the gestures, tools, and smells are the same as they were two thousand years ago. Squatting on the bare earth in front of a heap of branches, the men begin by cutting away the bark. The outer bark, thick and only faintly fragrant, is removed. Beneath this, against the wood, lies a thinner, lighter-colored bark in which the essential oils are concentrated. This is prised away in the same manner before being left to dry on racks under shelter for twenty-four hours. It is then placed inside a wooden cylinder and scratched with a knife so as to extract the phellem. Once this is done, the piece is a mere twenty-fifth of an inch thick. Cut into sections a foot long and

laid to dry once more for two days, it slowly rolls up, adopting its familiar tube-like appearance with its twin scrolls. To make an attractive, compact, and marvelously aromatic cinnamon stick, it remains to select four or five rolls of various sizes and fit them one into the other. All these operations create debris and bark trimmings which are collected to produce cinnamon powder.

In the West, cinnamon is no longer as popular as it was during the Middle Ages and is all too often restricted to the odd sweet dessert, such as rice pudding or apple cake, jams, or French toast—a dusting on golden-brown slices of bread—and to a few aromatic drinks, such as Spanish sangria. When André Lerch—the pastry-cook from Alsace who has been delighting Parisians for more than forty years—starts to talk of cinnamon, however, his eyes light up in a way that seems to guarantee that this cherished spice will never fall out of favor. Out of the 500 gm (18 ounces) of spice that he mixes for his spice bread, 14 are of a fine Ceylonese cinnamon freshly milled for him. This spice bread is thus above all a cinnamon bread with honey, flavored with a soupçon of clove, nutmeg, and anise. It is also cinnamon that warms his divine damson and apple tarts and that, back in his native Alsace, enriches blood sausage with a flavor at once invigorating and mild. The cuisines of a number of other countries also put the sweet yet intense aroma of cinnamon to good use in their savory dishes.

Of the two sorts of cinnamon—one from Sri Lanka, bold and strongly perfumed, and the other, rather spicier, from China (see page 49) known as cassia—Europeans tend to prefer the former, while Americans and the Chinese opt for the latter. Medieval Europe on the other hand employed both, since the dried cassia flowers resembling an oversized if only mildly aromatic clove bud were also much appreciated. Today they are found only in China. Unlike cassia, which is collected from cinnamon trees at least ten years old (above, in Sumatra), Ceylonese cinnamon is taken from shrubs which are regularly pruned to stunt their growth (facing page, photograph from early in the twentieth century). After harvest, the slender bark is laid out to dry.

789

Moroccan cooks appreciate the way cinnamon lightens fish dishes such as trout with dates, as well as mutton or lamb tajine, while a stick of cinnamon is also added during the preparation of a couscous bouillon. Cinnamon is most highly prized, however, in marvelous *pastillas*, delicate and irresistible flaky pastries, usually stuffed with pigeon and almonds and decorated with pretty intertwined patterns. In Asia, it is used to perfume the rice that cools the spicy meat. In India, it is added to many a *masala*, the spice mixtures that are commonly called "curries" in the West, most notably in *garam masala* to which we shall return. Vegetable and meat curries can both be improved by its mellow-

ness, as can numerous chutneys, tart condiments based on spiced vegetables or fruits candied in lemon juice or sweetened vinegar. Mango and quince chutneys fragrant with cinnamon can be used to enliven both rice dishes and broiled meats. Widely used in the United States, Chinese cassia also goes into the composition of a famous Chinese mix, the "five spices" (or "five powders"), used as a delicate flavoring for poultry. Cinnamon from Sri Lanka, at once milder and more subtle, is wonderful in tea, chocolate or coffee. The fruity taste of the better Arabica coffees is brought out all the better if, in place of the usual fattening sugar, a little piece of freshly milled cinnamon bark is stirred into it.

Chocolate first made the acquaintance of cinnamon on its arrival in Spain in the sixteenth century, and the two have remained firm friends ever since. All the finest chocolate-makers are fond of marrying the two flavors (above left, a large bar made by Bernachon of Lyon. Since the dawn of time in China and the fifteenth century in Europe, cinnamon has also been used to flavor traditional teabreads which, in addition, call for cloves, star anise or aniseed, and sometimes ginger, coriander or vanilla (right, a special spice-bread mix). One such specialty from Dijon, flavored solely with anise, is rather milder (facing page, a spice bread from the firm of Mulot and Petitjean).

Cardamom,
a most valuable seed

The seed of the cardamom is the only spice which arrives naturally sealed in a little packet–the dried fruit in which it is contained. This distinction epitomizes to perfection the select and delicate character of this minute brown grain, which, with ten or so companions, is held within a small oblong fruit around 1-2 cms (1/2 to 2/3 of an inch long). Together with saffron and vanilla, cardamom is the most costly spice, and of all the stronger spices it is also the mildest to the taste. Placed in the mouth, it yields a whole gamut of pleasurable sensations: first suck on it for a bit, the better to appreciate its velvety texture and sugary coating, then bite right through it to release a range of sublime flavors including lemon, camphor, and bergamot. It is an extraordinary mixture that lingers in the mouth, as if determined to conjure up images of the Cardamom Mountains from which it originally came.

THE CARDAMOM MOUNTAINS

It was probably among the wooded highlands sometimes known as the "Cardamom Mountains", between 1500 and 3000 feet up, where the monsoon rains fall lighter, that the little seeds of *Elettaria cardamomum* were first collected and eaten. These mountains in southwest India rise high above the plain of Kerala and the Malabar Coast, recognized as the most spice-rich region in the world (and one increasingly frequented by marvelling tourists). A network of paths snakes down the hills among the enormous tropical trees where songbirds nest. In the half-shade streaked with sunbeams, among the scented flowers and moss, clumps of longish, green and glittering leaves growing on tall stalks announce the treasure trove. At their base bloom splendid clusters of mauve and whitish-pink flowers which give place to fruits that resemble small shiny olives. Here grows the best cardamom in the world, whether wild or cultivated from rhizomes. The fruits can be collected from August to April by hand or with scissors, taking the greatest precautions so as not to damage the rest of the plant. The harvest must start at just the right time, when the green fruit is beginning to turn yellow. It is put into small buckets, then piled into jute sacks before being carted off to a processing plant.

First washed and then left to dry in the sun or else in drying-rooms at a low temperature, the fruit soon gives off a pervasive scent as well as starting to look like the furrowed and slightly knobby pale green capsules that are familiar. Good cardamom can be identified from the condition of these capsules, which must be tightly shut and green or green-amber in color, but never grayish.

It is in this form, as tiny, intact fruit, that cardamom is mainly marketed today: the capsule serves as a guarantee of the freshness and unadulterated nature of the seeds within. One has simply to free them with a fingernail or scissors. Before grinding or milling the seeds, it is best to roast them lightly in a skillet to release still more of their aroma. This cardamom, the most commonly available, is termed "green cardamom", while other fruits bleached in limewater give "white cardamom", considered by some to be more elegant, though the seeds inside have the same appearance and flavor as the green.

More scarce in the West is a third type of cardamom, "brown" or "black" cardamom,

Good green cardamom requires fastidious sorting (facing page, above, in India). Before being allowed into the kitchen, the little brown seeds–at once mild, slightly bitter, yet peppery–should remain hermetically sealed within their capsule (below). In Indian cooking, where cardamom predominates in many spice mixes, the capsule is also used unopened to flavor the water in which rice is cooked, for example. Strongly scented, true cardamom is an ideal spice for giving added depth to low-fat recipes. In his *Grande cuisine allégée,* chef André Gaüzère suggests an aromatic savory lamb charlotte with cardamom, amounting to a mere 255 calories.

highly prized in India and Indonesia for its woody and smoky aroma reminiscent of mushrooms: its fruit, from another variety native to China, is dark brown in color and the size of a walnut. In some grocery stores, it is possible to find ready-ground cardamom; this is to be avoided since it rapidly turns stale if it is not carefully stored.

CARDAMOM AND COFFEE

For all those who enjoy traveling in the Orient, the exceptional fragrance of cardamom irresistibly evokes Indian cooking—of which it is one of the essential ingredients—and also coffee as served in the many Arab countries where it is used generously as a flavoring, particularly in Egypt. In India, it is used in ground form as part of numerous spice mixes or *masalas*; as intact capsules, it flavors both rice and meat dishes. It is the heart and soul of the staggering *kulfi*, a delicious ice-cream combining cardamom and pistachio. It can also be served after dessert in seed form, accompanying a little dish of betel nut (the fruit of the areca betel palm, which can be used to make cachous), aniseed and fennel seeds, fruit pits and sugar crystals, in the sophisticated digestive-cum-breath-freshener known as *pan masala*. Cardamom enjoys the virtue of completely eliminating unwelcome aftertastes, especially garlic.

Transported from the Indian coast to the Persian Gulf aboard *dhows*, green cardamom reigned over the Orient two thousand years ago. It is now found in every spice mix in Lebanese, Syrian, and Egyptian cuisine, flavoring meat and fish dishes alike. Yet in the Middle East, it is in coffee that it reigns supreme, as described by the poet Mahmoud Darwich in *Une Mémoire pour l'oubli*: "a single spoonful of coffee amplified by the aroma of cardamom floated unhurriedly onto the seething water..." In Egypt, as in Lebanon, ground cardamom from Guatemala is added to the water while the coffee is being prepared, or else the ground coffee is sold ready flavored. Among the Bedouin, a cardamom capsule is traditionally placed into the spout of the pot before pouring out the coffee. In the Yemen, cardamom is used with ginger to flavor the traditional drink, *qishr*, a decoction of coffee fruit. For centuries, coffee and cardamom have enjoyed a perfect love marriage founded on the harmony of their fruity flavors and an even balance between bitterness and mildness. In Europe, only the Anglo-Saxons and the Scandinavians receive cardamom so warmly. In Scandinavia, it is used generously to flavor biscuits and above all brioches in all shapes and sizes to be enjoyed at teatime. The Swedes are still the keenest consumers of cardamom in Europe, partly, no doubt, because it is readily incorporated into their *aqua vitae*. On Christmas Eve, finely crushed cardamom is used to decorate and flavor a cocktail mousse, *mumma*, a mixture of stout, port, vodka, and lemonade made at home to be drunk with herring or salmon. In France, too, great chefs are now beginning exalt the flavor of cardamom: Alain Passard in his Paris restaurant *L'Arpège*, for example, serves a sublime but simple dessert of coffee sorbet with cardamom, accompanying a vanilla ice-cream: three tastes joining forces to create an ode to pleasure.

Chocolate-makers and pastry-cooks have only recently been won over by cardamom. The great patissier Pierre Hermé, for example, now flavors some of his coffee- or orange-based desserts with it. Similar in taste to green cardamom, white cardamom (facing page) is simply the green type artificially bleached. In India, it is considered more attractive. Brown cardamom, on the other hand (right), comes from a different variety of Chinese origin. Its camphor-like, smoky flavor means that it is confined to strong, salty dishes, such as game.

Clove, a bud
from the southern isles

Clove is the perfume of Indonesia. The two most intense sensations that greet the traveler on first setting foot in the archipelago are the sweltering tropical heat and the heady aroma of clove. This is because it is well-nigh certain that, not far off, an Indonesian is smoking a *kretek*, a cigarette of brown tobacco blended generously with crushed cloves. Throughout any journey in the islands, this sweet scent, a combination of fleshy red berries and peppery carnation, will follow you. If you find it irresistible, you can always make a stop-over on the island of Ambon in the Moluccas, the cradle of history for the clove.

FROM TREE TO CLOVE

From a distance, the island that was the birthplace of the clove, with its luxuriant vegetation, its irregular relief and its coconut palms lining sandy creeks, still looks like a sort of abandoned Treasure Island. But once on land, it becomes clear just how much the inhabitants love and care for their island, and how proud they are of their clove trees. They will happily invite you to enter a plantation, convinced that you will soon be fascinated by the beauty of the trees and their extraordinary scent. Standing almost forty feet high, the *Eugenia caryophyllata* unfurls a magnificent canopy of glossy green leaves that form a quivering pyramid centered around a light-gray trunk. The graceful leaves exude

an aromatic oil which transforms the whole plantation into a scented paradise, more highly perfumed still in the flowering months. The blossoms are never allowed to open, however: the four-petaled white flowers of the little clove rarely see the light of day, since it is as buds that they have the most fragrance and hence are picked, later to be sold whole. The foremost quality required of a picker is sharp eyesight: the trees are large, and only the buds about to mature are harvested, just as they begin to turn pink. One or two days later, they would lose something of their aromatic essence. Cropping is done by hand. Women and children work on the lower branches while the men clamber up into the trees or else use long bamboo-cane poles to dislodge the topmost flowers.

The freshly picked pink bud has the shape of a nail: the pointed tip is formed by the tube of the calyx, with four sepals grasping the "head", the round nodule formed by the four petals closing around the stamens and pistil. At this point, the bud is still supported by the peduncle, and the first task—lengthy and painstaking—is to detach it by hand. The buds are then laid out on matting and placed in the sun to dry for three days. The same process is followed on the island of Zanzibar, where the clove was introduced in 1818, and which has since, with its small sister island of Pemba, become the world's largest producer of cloves.

Contained in its essential oils, the aromatic extract of the clove is so wonderfully pungent that it is found not only in the world's best cuisine: numerous perfumes today, such as "L'Air du Temps" by Nina Ricci and "Armani pour Homme", contain a few drops of this remarkable oil, often mixed with ylang-ylang to give a floral note of carnation, at once fresh and sensual. But in the fragrant plantations of Indonesia (above), Grenada (facing page), Zanzibar and India, everything starts with the meticulous harvest, the "paring", and selection (following page) of the bud which, for the sake of our pleasure, will never be allowed to open. Once dried, the clove may be used to stud an onion to flavor the traditional French beef stew, *pot-au-feu* (page 79).

The same is true of other producers on the island of Penang in Malaysia and also on the Comoros where, thanks to careful gathering and drying, the cloves are frequently of exceptional quality.

AN EXTRAORDINARY OIL

Since time immemorial, cloves have been used for purifying and antiseptic purposes. The essential oil that impregnates it, and its principal ingredient, eugenol, possess genuine and acknowledged anti-bacterial, anti-fungal, and analgesic properties that are utilized to this day in dentistry. But the clove and its remarkable oil are used above all to enrich numerous traditional dishes in both West and East with their spicy, bitter and fruity flavor. Since clove blends extremely well with other spices—such as ginger, peppercorn, and cardamom—it is always found in Indian *masalas* and Chinese spice mixes. In India, it is used to pep up the flavor of quids of betel, based on leaves from a variety of pepper and pieces of betel nut, which serve as a kind of stimulant gum that can be chewed for hours. Cloves may heighten the seasoning of *court-bouillons* and marinades, or—stuck in an onion—of beef stews, or else be used to stud a ham. Cloves also feature in sauerkraut and in that irresistible hotpot from Alsace with its three different meats baked in an oven, the *baëckeofe*. In Scandinavia, cloves provide the seasoning to soused herring and the headcheese pâté that is eaten traditionally at Christmastime. As for desserts

and sweet treats, cloves often serve to add a dash of warmth to apple desserts.

In her classic *Spices, Salt and Aromatics in the English Kitchen*, the distinguished culinary writer Elizabeth David advised against the traditional use of whole cloves in apple pie—"their main destination in the English kitchen"—since "they spoil the taste". Milled, however, cloves remain indispensable in Christmas pudding, mincemeat, and hot cross buns. Roger Vergé, another clove enthusiast and first-rate chef, suggests grating a little into lemon or orange juice, the resulting layers of flavor proving quite delicious. Cloves may be used ground or grated, but should always be purchased whole, as pre-milled they easily lose their flavor. They should be stored separately in a hermetically-sealed container, at room temperature and out of direct light. In stores, you occasionally come across cloves that have ripened too long on the tree or have been overdried and thus have lost a considerable part of their quality. Always make sure that the pointed tip of the clove is a rosy brown, that the head adheres firmly to the shaft, and that a smear of oil oozes out when it is scratched with a fingernail. Once all these conditions are satisfied, on an icy winter's day when your bones—and perhaps your very soul—are frozen through, toss a few cloves into some mulled wine (a little Bandol, perhaps, with a touch of cinnamon) and rejoin the land of the living.

Once the "nail head" of the clove has formed after drying (above), it is at last ready to dispense its many beneficial qualities. It is shown here studding a whole orange to make a pomander which will impart a delicate fragrance to clothes in a wardrobe or to fresh laundry. It can also be used to add the finishing note to an original pot-pourri (facing page, clove-studded orange pomander, part of the "perfume bouquet" available from the Paris florist "Les Milles Feuilles"). In the Middle Ages, fruit such as apples stuck with cloves were carried as a protection against the plague (Queen Elizabeth I was to continue the tradition). As far as taste is concerned, cloves harmonize particularly well with oranges and lemons, for example in these spiced candied oranges (facing page, in their glass jar) which complement duck, pork, and game.

Cumin and Caraway:
a sun for each hemisphere

On winter days, when from my window the Paris roofscape and the sky are cemented together in an unbroken and cheerless gray, it is enough for me to sniff a good pinch of cumin to be transported back to Cairo's great souk, the Khan-el-Khalili. Well before you reach the quarter around the Al Azhar mosque, exhalations of *kamun* waft through the air, overpowering all other smells and heralding the magic of the souk itself, with its colorful profusion of spices. And it is just as warming to breathe in the aroma of caraway, a seed so similar to cumin that the two are often confused. Indeed, these two spices are such close relations that we have decided to treat them together.

FROM MOROCCO TO INDIA
Cumin, the queen of spices in the eastern Mediterranean, loves to soak up the sun. It is the little fruit of a plant around a foot high, *Cuminum cyminum*, which sets its pale pink flowers in graceful umbels on frail stalks that undulate in the warm breeze. Cumin displays a marked fondness for the Mediterranean over every other sea. It is cultivated on all its coasts, from Morocco to Egypt and from Syria to Spain, and it also thrives under the sunny skies of Iran and India. Each summer the tiny flowers wither and fall, making way for bunches of seeds that are allowed to ripen for a short time

before being cut off at the stalk. Once dried for a few days, the clusters are gently shaken to knock out the seeds, which are then carefully screened and sorted. Measuring around 5 millimeters (1/5 inch) long, they are generally greenish brown, or more rarely light beige or almost black in color, and deeply gouged.

Warm and potent, hardly spicy at all, with a distinct tang of aniseed and lemon, cumin is a generous seasoning. Since the time of the ancient Egyptians and the Assyrians—its aroma has fallen out of favor in the medieval West except in southern regions, where the plant continued to be cultivated in gardens. In northern and eastern Europe it nonetheless remained in certain recipes for flavored bread. Delicious bagels—those small, soft, and round rolls that were already a Jewish specialty throughout central Europe before invading the United States—are often sprinkled with some little brown seeds, as are the pretzels, flute baguettes and savory croissants of Alsace. Indeed, from Morocco and Egypt to India, the rich scent of cumin hovers over many a great dish.

In North Africa, cumin is also to be found in the fiery harissa that accompanies couscous, while in Egypt it is the predominant spice in seasoning mixes. In the wonderful cuisine of Syria it is used in the traditional walnut,

In the thirteenth-century BC ruins of a merchant's stall in Mycenae, archeologists have unearthed a clay tablet containing a list of aromatics, among them cumin. Used frequently in the Orient, in the West the warmth of cumin (facing page) provides a fine accompaniment to potato salad or sautéed vegetables–zucchini, cauliflower or brussels sprouts. The Troisgros brothers conceived the splendid idea of flavoring their veal chops with it, accompanied by a dot of harissa. As for caraway (above), its slightly aniseed and fruity flavor–traditionally used to impart mildness to Munster cheese and to several kinds of *charcuterie*–is also marvelous in sweet dishes: at Saint-Rémy-de-Provence in southern France, the chocolatier Joël Durand has created a recipe for an exquisite hot chocolate using ground caraway seeds. In Morocco, it is used ground to flavor tajines and enters into the composition of *m'hammer*, a traditional and relatively mild red sauce in which meat or chicken is simmered.

cumin, and pomegranate juice sauce that is served with meat and vegetables alike. As in Lebanon, it also flavors many succulent types of *mezze*, such as stuffed cabbage leaves and falafels, which are some of the gastronomic treasures of the region. Farther to the north, cumin also reigns supreme in Turkish cooking, where it is an indispensable ingredient of *köfte* (spiced meat balls). After passing through Iran, where it becomes a charming addition to sweetened rice or rice and green cabbage recipes, cumin reaches its favored land, India. Here it serves as a base for many spice mixes, and of course in the most common of the them all, the *garam masala*, which is used as much in curries as in the flame-cooked dishes prepared in the traditional *tandoor* oven. In the sublime cuisine of India (where it is often black in color), cumin is also one of the spices that can be quickly pan-roasted before use so as to release its seasoning qualities. In fact, this is a practice to be recommended for any recipe, Indian or otherwise, especially when the cumin is to be used in ground form. In Mexico, cumin is the favorite spice next to chili peppers and is used as a flavoring in many dishes. The highly popular *encebollado* sauce, for example, made from chopped onions and tomatoes, fresh coriander and cumin and served as an accompaniment to meat or rice, derives all its savor from cumin.

CARAWAY, SUN OF THE NORTH
A botanical cousin of cumin, caraway (*Carum*

carvi) is cultivated in the Netherlands and in central Europe, as well as in India. The little caraway seed is often mistaken for cumin, though its taste is not as long-lasting and it is slightly milder, even a touch lemony. The seed is also rather smaller and is recognizable above all by its color, almost black, and its gently curved shape. It is often said that cumin is a hot-country spice and caraway a cold-country one, which would be true enough were it not for the fact that caraway is found in North African and Indian cuisine, occasionally flavoring harissa and *masala*. But it remains the case that caraway, with its dash of aniseed, is primarily used to give extra glow to northern Europe recipes—first and foremost in breads, whether in Irish soda bread or German rye bread such as pumpernickel. Then come the *charcuterie* of the north, particularly the cabbage dishes of Scandinavia, such as sauerkraut, and cheeses, primarily Gouda and Munster (often wrongly thought to be flavored with cumin), which it renders mellow and tangy. A sprinkling of caraway also lends a hint of warmth to the delicious soft smoked cheese so loved by the Danes, *Fynsk rygeost*. Without caraway, a certain something would be missing from Jamaica cake, as well as from countless sweet and savory biscuits. Finally, we would also be without the delectable grain alcohol misleadingly known as *kümmel* (from "cumin" in German, though it is caraway that gives its fruity taste) which aids the digestion of such delicacies.

Juniper (above), a small, brownish, bitter-tasting berry with a pine-like scent is not surprisingly redolent of the gin that is made from it. Like caraway seeds, juniper berries lend a pleasant flavoring to sauerkraut, pork, and pâtés of northern European countries and in Alsace. It should be slightly crushed before use. Close to both cumin and caraway, the blue-black seeds of the poppy (facing page) are also sprinkled over many types of bread, most notably in eastern Europe (insert, cumin and poppy seed breads). Ground poppy seeds also enhance pastries with a light flavor of hazelnut. As the seed is extremely tough, special mills have been designed in Germany to process them.

Ginger,
the root of pleasure

Ginger is the only spice that you can actually sink your teeth into. In its purest and most deliciously sweltering state, this spice–which lured many a medieval gourmet to sinful gluttony–is a baroque tuber with a multitude of knobby protuberances, sometimes called "fingers", and a rough skin the color of metallic linen, the bizarre rhizome of a plant of Asian origin, *Zingiber officinalis.* Lovers of strong flavors can simply slice thin, slightly fibrous rounds that will melt on the tongue with a subtle taste of camphor and lemony pepperiness. There are those, of course, who entertain the hope that it will spur them on to other pleasures...

"IN OLD AGE, IT AWAKENS LOVE"
The fact that the word *ginger*, by a series of twists and turns via Persia and Greece, derives ultimately from the Sanskrit word *srngavera* ("horn-shaped") is a clear indication that the tuber has been known and used since the dawn of history. The Chinese, very early on, were already drinking a tea made from a decoction of crushed tea leaves and ginger. Widespread in Asia, it began to arrive in the West around the first century AD, though it only became popular throughout Europe during the Crusades of the Middle Ages. Such was its triumph at this point that it supplanted even pepper to become the most widely used spice in the kitchen. So deliciously sour and warming was it that no self-respecting dish was complete without a generous proportion, particularly in thick bouillons, stews, and brothy soups. Certainly it was less costly than

pepper, and it possessed a piquancy that was just as delicious. Moreover it also enjoyed a reputation not merely as a stimulant but also as a powerful aphrodisiac. Around the twelfth century, Arab and Jewish scholars at the prestigious Italian school of medicine at Salerno were all in agreement on this property, summed up in one treatise in the following quaint quatrain: "Over a cold in the stomach, kidney, or lung / Fiery Ginger always has the upper hand. / Quenching the thirst, it enlivens and excites the brain / While in old age, it awakens a youthful, new-found love.

A CATHEDRAL OF GOURMET DELIGHTS
By the end of the thirteenth century, Europeans knew where ginger came from thanks to Marco Polo's *Divisament dou Monde*, in which it frequently makes an appearance by the roadside in India and China. Today, its geography appears far more complex, for it is cultivated in virtually all the world's tropical regions, as well as in China, Jamaica, Nigeria, Sri Lanka, and Sierra Leone. Indeed it requires nothing more than fertile soil, sun, a warm climate, considerable amounts of water–and a good deal of constant care. Planted in rows before the rainy season, trimmings from rhizomes from the previous year's harvest are left to develop for six to ten months. These fields need frequent hoeing and the shoots must be cut back to encourage the precious tuber to swell. A few weeks prior to harvesting, a field of ginger does not make a particularly prepossessing sight: the plants resemble a sort of reed standing over three

The ginger rhizome (facing page, above left and below right, with a Japanese wooden grater) imparts its piquant, peppery flavor to a wide range of gastronomic recipes from the world over. At the Hôtel Crillon in Paris, chef Christian Constant uses it to flavor his puff-pastry *croustillant* of calves' sweetbreads and crawfish. Less elaborately, ginger can lend an exotic touch to a "*pot-au-feu*" beef stew or to a *boeuf bourguignon*, to fruit salads or to stewed fruit. From the same family, galingale (facing page, upper right, the root; the fruit below left), adds its fiery yet acidic notes to Asian cuisine: sliced and dried it is often to be found–along with lemon grass–in delicious Thai soups. Following double page spread: ginger drying in Kerala, India.

feet high, sporting a panoply of long, tapering, sword-shaped leaves.

Generally, the harvest starts once the leaves begin to fade. The rhizomes are very carefully dug up with a fork-like tool to avoid damaging them. Transferred to a processing plant, they then undergo several days of painstaking preparation: first they are sorted and washed in boiling water, then they are laid out on matting to dry in the sun for three or four days. This is the method for the most common type of ginger, known as "fresh ginger".

From time immemorial ginger lovers have always known how to vary their pleasures, and for them there also exists dried ginger (often sold ready-ground), prepared from rhizomes that have been left to ripen for a longer time (nine or ten months) before cropping. While it is less fragrant than fresh ginger, the flavor it imparts to a dish is distinctly more *piquant*, and thus it has become an essential ingredient in the preparation of some of the hottest Indian mixes.

In addition to spice mixes, the full rich flavor of this pungent tuber may be appreciated in the grandest of recipes. If it is to be eaten fresh, the tuber should have a pleasantly firm appearance with a skin that is irregular but never shriveled. To reveal its flavor, peel just

an inch or two and grate it onto a green salad with a vinaigrette or into a sweetened fruit salad: the sharp acidity of ginger can enhance the sweet as much as the savory, and it is as valuable for spicing up a duck (for a change from orange or turnips, for example) as for jam or stewed fruit. All fruits marry well with ginger, and most particularly banana, pineapple, and melon. For sauces and slow-cooked dishes, add a few slivers of ginger crushed in a mortar or with a knife blade, removing them before serving. Ginger juice may be squeezed with a garlic press and trickled into a sauce or vinaigrette dressing.

There is also preserved ginger (candied in syrup) and crystallized (stem) ginger (boiled in syrup and rolled in sugar), presented in little pieces which have been served as a tasty tidbit for centuries. Both are exceedingly spicy and slightly bitter-tasting—perfect for injecting a little pep into a long, slow afternoon.

The British—enviable masters at finding agreeable ways of passing their leisure hours—have erected a veritable gourmet cathedral to ginger, the keystones of which are gingerbread (for a snack at teatime), numerous biscuits, tarts, cakes, and jams, as well as chewing gum and a whole range of alcoholic drinks, including the famous ginger ale. The Chinese are also great lovers of ginger, especially candied in syrup. As for the Japanese, they too have a soft spot for it, grating it with special little wooden graters. Most *sushi* enthusiasts cannot fully appreciate their raw fish and rice without *wasabi*, a sort of horseradish, or *gari*, flesh-pink slivers of ginger marinated in sweetened vinegar, eaten separately between mouthfuls of *sushi*. Less fiery and fibrous than normal fresh ginger, the milder *gari* variety is prepared from very young, undried tubers.

The Japanese venerate the tenderest, pinkest ginger in the form of the incredibly mild gari (above); in China, ginger may be preserved in a sugary syrup to make a melt-in-the-mouth treat. In Britain, dried and ground, it is used to flavor a host of drinks, cakes, biscuits (facing page, ginger in all its forms, including organic biscuits of the Duchy brand created by the Prince of Wales in 1990, the proceeds of which go towards protecting the environment). The food historian Elizabeth David, in her excellent book on spices in English cooking, recalls also the old tradition of serving ginger with melon "to counteract the chilling effects of the melon".

Enchanting
nutmeg

Nutmeg has only to give off its gentle fragrance of mint and bergamot, hinting at its delicately warm yet agreeably bitter and lemony flavor in order to seduce us. It possesses qualities verging on the ecstatic in combination with the sublime taste of a plate of mashed potatoes–the variety known as *rattes* for example–with Robuchon cheese and a slathering of butter. However, this enchanting nut also harbors a secret weapon, in the form of a substance that is believed to be both hallucinogenic and aphrodisiac when taken in high doses, such as the colossal quantities contained in the highly toxic pills known as "Ecstasy" or "X". It goes without saying that a pinch of grated nutmeg contains only an infinitesimal amount of this substance, and carries no dangerous side-effects. But once tasted, nutmeg can nevertheless prove addictive...

during that period. Nutmeg grows everywhere on these islands: handsome trees, standing around thirty or forty feet high, with dense green foliage with tints of gold, bear flowers and fruits throughout the year. The scent of the little yellow or pale green flowers hangs heavy in the air, while the fruits, around the size of a small apple, turn from green to ivory yellow.

Once ripe, the fruits split in two to reveal the treasure within: a brown stone cradled in a deep red membrane like a piece of loose-weave netting, called the "aril", or mace. On the best plantations, the ripe fruits are not allowed to fall, in order to prevent risk of damage to the mace.

Three times a year, therefore, pickers harvest them with the traditional *gai gai*, a bamboo cane equipped with a little hoop-net at one end that can contain around a dozen fruits. These are then emptied into a wicker basket slung over the shoulder.

A little way off in the distance, under an awning stretching the length of a large, white building, a group of men and women seated on the bare earth are busy with the nuts that have already been extracted from the fruit. Here the work consists of very carefully separating the nutmeg from the mace with a knife. The mace is then placed on a huge round wickerwork tray, where it will be sun-dried for several days, changing in color gradually from red to an

NUTMEG AND MACE

Nutmeg grows today on several Indonesian islands, in India and on Sri Lanka, and principally on the island of Grenada. Here, the spice is such an important part of the country's economy that it appears on the national flag. On the islands of Banda, where it has always been cultivated, the cruelties of colonialism are commemorated in a traditional dance, in which dancers wearing the uniforms of Portuguese or Dutch officers, act out the atrocities perpetrated

There is no more beautiful fruit than that from the nutmeg tree (above), especially when its fruit have opened. The red-colored mace that surrounds the nut must be dislodged delicately (facing page, in Indonesia, and following page, on Grenada). The seed kernel–the nutmeg proper–is a subtle spice, with a sharp flavor of hazelnut. Its full delicacy may be appreciated, as described by Colette in *The Evening Star*, in "melting knuckles of pork, cooked in casserole [...] moistened with their gravy flavored by a little celery, a little nutmeg." As for mace (p. 95), still more intense in flavor, the late and much-missed supplier of fine foods Paul Corcellet used it to sprinkle it over a simple dish of fresh peas.

Macis

orangey brown. It is in this form that it is presented, or later ground and sold as a powder. The dried filaments give off a slightly woody aroma which is richer still than that of the nut, or nutmeg, while on the palate, a lemony, more acidic and full-bodied note predominates.

The nut, meanwhile, is laid to dry on ricks for about a week. Once the kernel—the nutmeg proper—moves freely inside when the nut is shaken, the outer shell is broken with a wooden mallet. In past centuries, the Dutch used to drench the nutmegs in lime water before exporting them, in order to prevent them from germinating and thus endangering their monopoly. The custom has remained, and the kernels are still washed in this way, causing their color to lighten perceptibly. They are then left to dry for two or three weeks before being graded by size and brought to market.

Virtually any dish, savory or sweet, can be improved by adding a pinch of nutmeg or some fine shavings of mace. As well as being richer in taste, mace is often preferred by cooks to nutmeg since it affects less of a change of color in certain dishes, white sauce being a prime example. Nutmeg grated on mashed potatoes, spinach, or in a béchamel sauce are considered the great classics in the West. It has the ability to transform a simple and otherwise dull cheese soufflé, while a quick flourish of the grater can bring about the same transformation to thick vegetable soups.

The merest pinch or the faintest trace brings with it all the exotic flavors of faraway islands. Nutmeg enriches a modest fried egg, while its hints of citrus and mint join equally well in harmony with fruit, orange fruit salads or chocolate mousse. It complements wine and other alcoholic drinks. Toulouse-Lautrec, for example, was never without a piece of nutmeg and a little grater to spice the port that he drank to such excess. In the past, nutmeg was habitually added to mulled wine and beer. Even now, the finest barmen—such as the highly respected Bertrand Merlette at the Hotel Raphaël in Paris—often spice up their alexandras (a cocktail based on milk or crème fraîche, cognac and cocoa powder) with a dash of nutmeg.

In the East, both nutmeg and mace are important ingredients in many a mixture of spices. But whatever the dish, only whole fresh nutmeg should be used, grated finely or ground in a special nutmeg mill. Powdered nutmeg tends to go stale quickly and runs the risk of being adulterated. In the same way, whole mace is far more worthwhile than ground: difficult to grate, it should be pounded in a small mortar. If you have the choice, go for the larger nuts, both riper and tastier, as recommended by the fourteenth-century cookbook, *Le Ménagier de Paris* : "The heaviest nutmegs are always the best."

In past centuries, nutmeg (above, the kernel in its broken shell) was so popular in Europe that it was not unusual for people to carry their own little grater (facing page). Some were of silver, especially in England, where traveling chests—as the collector Elizabeth B. Miles notes in a charming little book—were always equipped with a knife, fork, spoon, spice box, and nutmeg grater. Asian countries are not content simply with ground nutmeg: nutmeg oil, which can be made into a powerful antiseptic balm and stomach medecine, is a common remedy, applied externally like clove oil to relieve many ailments (following double page spread).

Piments, chilis
et paprikas

One of the most splendid scenes one can hope to encounter when traveling off the beaten track in the Mexican, Indian, or Chinese countryside is a village house hung with bunches of shiny, tapering fruit of a vibrant red color: these are peppers drying in the sun. In France, the same spectacle can be admired in the Basque country, the kingdom of the Espelette capsicum. In the area around the little village of the same name cradled in an inland valley, they have been producing an exceptionally fruity pepper for four centuries. It is used to season *garbure*–a wonderfully thick cabbage hotpot with a confit of goose–as well as with the local mouth-watering farm-produced Bayonne ham.

THE ESPELETTE PEPPER FIESTA
Every year in the village of Espelette on the last Sunday of October after Mass, the *Chevaliers de la Confrérie du Piment*–the "Knights of the Brotherhood of the Espelette Pepper"–gather around the grand master in front of the medieval castle to receive new members. The solemnity of the ceremony is highlighted by the knights' costume: the traditional Basque beret, a magnificent bottle-green suit and a great deep-red *collier*. The town of Espelette has been celebrating since the previous evening. The village dance and pelota match–played against a wall like American handball–have already taken place in celebration of the pepper harvest. On Sunday, the village streets, thronged by thousands of visitors mingling among the producers' stalls, are all decorated with ropes of peppers.

Folklore apart, Espelette's magnificent and delicious red capsicum is the end result of the remarkable efforts of some thirty farmers from an area covering eight local districts. For although this pepper may be only a *Capsicum annum* like all other peppers termed "sweet" or "bell", it possesses a distinctively straight and regular shape and a sweet, fruity taste found nowhere else in the world. This is the result of a combination of slightly acid local soil, a warm southerly wind that prolongs summer until the end of November, and frequent rains from the nearby mountains.

Work begins in March, when the seeds are sown on a warm layer of humus and manure. After germination, the shoots are pricked out into clods of earth, where they are left to grow for two months before being transplanted in the fields. The first ripe peppers, around four inches long and only partly red, appear in mid-August. Cropping, which is carried out entirely by hand, can now begin; it lasts ten weeks, until the first sign of cold. Back at the farm, the capsicums are sorted by hand and any damaged, split or blackened peppers discarded. Some are sent to the market to be sold loose. Others are threaded on strings to be sold as handsome red clusters, or are hung to dry on the white house fronts, sometimes covering them completely. Each string is threaded with at least twenty fruit, adding a dash of brilliant color to a kitchen as well as transforming the outside of a house. As the peppers slowly dry and continue to ripen, they may be taken off one by one, to be cut into shreds and tossed in a sauce, for example, towards the end of cooking, or perhaps sprinkled over a salad. But in the small holdings of Espelette, after two months drying in the sun, the strings are

In his island idyll in *Paul et Virginie*, Bernardin de Saint-Pierre describes peppers with "blood-red pods brighter than any coral". A string of this most dazzling of all spices is proudly displayed by an experienced and distinguished producer from Espelette, Xan Nobilat (facing page). The sweet peppers cultivated in this small Basque village and the surrounding region are of such outstanding quality that they have recently been awarded the status of "Appellation d'Origine Contrôlée"–like the vintages of the finer French vineyards. In addition to its traditional Basque uses, the sunny fruitiness of this little capsicum often sold in powdered form can best be appreciated with all white meats, fish and vegetables that call for a delicate note of spiciness.

placed in a baker's oven to complete the process even more thoroughly: the capsicums are then crushed before being sold as a thick, bright orange powder which adds a dash of sunshine to any recipe.

PEPPERS CONQUER THE WORLD

For the Basque country, our story begins in the sixteenth century, when a Spaniard brought a few seeds of pimiento back from the New World. The species is native to America and the West Indies, where in 1493 Christopher Colombus himself first stumbled upon it on the island of Hispaniola. Not long afterwards, Cortés and his men feared they were in danger of catching fire when they first drunk chocolate served by the Aztecs, well doused with hot peppers. There the fiery red fruit was known by the name of chili, and this name is still used to designate the family of small and extremely spicy capsicums from hotter climates (*Capsicum frutescens*). Archeological excavations have revealed that peppers have been eaten in Mexico for nine thousand years. From the oblong-shaped green pepper, the *serrano*, to the deep red dried *ancho*, by way of the fiery green *habañero*—used to make the popular *salsa verde*—or the milder and fruity *pasado*, the Mexicans use a hundred varieties to pep up guacamole, beans and stews, including *mole poblano*, a dish combining poultry, chocolate and peppers which goes back to the time of the ancient Mayan civilizations. Three different pepper varieties are used for this recipe: the *ancho*, the spicier *mulato* and the exceptionally hot and almost black *pasilla*. Whole, the *pasilla* measures some six inches long and is

Chilies have been eaten in Mexico for nine thousand years. A hundred or so varieties with differing degrees of fieriness and of virtually all shapes and colors are used in a considerable number of cooked recipes, or else simply served at the table in a sauce. Some pepper sauces are destined for specific dishes, such as pork and beans seasoned with a very salty mixture of strong green pepper and tomato, or barbecues and dried meats enlivened with a *salsa borracha* ("drunken sauce"), containing a strong chili (the *serrano*), garlic, onion, cheese, *pulque* (the fermented juice of maguey or agave), and olive oil.

often eaten stuffed with beef, thinly sliced sweet peppers, fresh coriander, and onion.

The most common use of chili peppers in Mexico, however, is the spicy sauce known as salsa. On every table, whether at home or in a restaurant, a bowl or small jar of sauce stands beside the salt cellar and the pepper mill. Green or red, depending on the variety of chili used, incorporating—according to the recipe—tomatoes, garlic, coriander and onions, a salsa will deliver its daily dose of fire to hors d'oeuvres and meat dishes.

Brought back to Europe from America at the same time as chocolate, peppers began their triumphant conquest of the globe in the sixteenth century. In Galician Spain, a fiesta is still held to celebrate the harvest of the minuscule and mild green chili pepper called the *pimiento del Padrón*, which is delicious when eaten fried. The

Spanish Basque country boasts a lively dish of "cod in spicy tomatoes *à la* Bay of Biscay"– *bacalao a la vizcaína*–with a fiery sauce bursting with a dozen *choriceros*, sweet and dry peppers that are also used to add spice to the famous *chorizo* sausages. Catalonia produces its *nioras*, round, red peppers used in almond and garlic salad dressings. All over Spain, broiled fish and meat are accompanied by little chilies macerated in vinegar, or by *romescu* sauce, made with *romesco* peppers, almonds and pine nuts. Mild peppers also add flavor to traditional garlic soup, to breadcrumb-based *migas*, to the gaspacho of La Mancha, and to the paella of Valencia.

Gradually, capsicums reached Greece and Turkey, while during the Ottoman era it became one of the foremost gastronomic specialties in Hungary, now home to a particular variety of *Capsicum annuum*, or mild paprika, a red cap-

A member of the sweet pepper family like the Espelette pepper, the round and red *niora* (or *ñora*) is a Spanish pimiento also found in North Africa, where it adds piquancy to salads and to many fish dishes. Another deliciously fruity pimiento from Spain appreciated in the Basque country–especially in Bilbao–is the long, red, and exquisitely mild *piquillo*, traditionally used to season cod *a la vizcaina*. It is also served in salads, cooked in sliced rounds with a little garlic, or stuffed whole with prawns and béchamel sauce before being browned over a low heat. Following double page spread: an assortment of peppers–among them capsicums and masalas–some American mixes ready-made for TexMex cooking and a traditional Jamaican sauce.

sicum which is the national spice and is always used in powdered form.

The Hungarians are unique in having a choice of sixteen different varieties of paprika, either from the region around Szeged or from Kalocsa in the south. The various "vintages" are graded into eight categories, from the "non-spicy" used predominantly for its color to the blazing "spicy", via the most common, the "extra-mild". Sun- or oven-dried then powdered, these paprikas are used generously to season and color virtually every dish, especially blushing Hungarian soups. Whole spoonfuls of the "extra-mild" are used to season Hungarian goulash, potatoes, ragouts, vegetable, meat and fish dishes, ewe's-milk cheeses and more.

The Portuguese and Arabs introduced much hotter varieties into Africa, capable of imparting flavor even to boiled *manioc*. The best-known African hot pepper is the infernal *pili-pili* widespread in a number of countries including Senegal and Guinea. Pounded together with the pulp of tomato and squash seeds, it is the basis for the spicy condiment-cum-sauce *rougail* and for many sauces added to semolina and meat dishes. In North Africa, a similar type of hot pepper is combined with garlic to make harissa; in Morocco it is used in a number of tajines. Asia, too, was overrun by the hot pepper at an early date, introduced by European and Arab colonists and travelers.

The burning hot *Capsicum frutescens* also reigns supreme in India, where production outstrips that of any other spice; indeed it is held in such high regard by many Indians that they are not prepared to admit to its foreign origins. It is the essential ingredient in chutneys and masalas and, of course, in all the shop-sold "chili powder" preparations that contain both hot and sweet peppers, in addition to cumin, clove, marjoram, and garlic. This explosive powder, found throughout Asia, is distinctly more fiery than the Mexican concoction of the same name.

Further to the east, the cuisines of Indonesia (whose hot pepper, *lombok*, is one of the world's most "extreme") and of Thailand make heavy use of spicy fried rice. In the Chinese province of Szechwan, pepper is a god to which sacrifice is made three times daily—at every meal: at breakfast, a bowl of noodles sprinkled with invigorating hot pepper is eaten, a traditional dish believed to ensure long life. Thus, when the great dissident writer Pa Kin celebrated his ninety-fourth birthday in November 1997, the Chinese—used to reading between the lines of the official press—when informed that the veteran writer had "eaten some noodles with peppers", inferred that his intellectual faculties

In African, Asian and West Indian cooking, flaming hot peppers are the preferred variety (above, Asian green peppers and "bonda a Man Jacques" from the West Indies). Fresh, dried, in combination or powdered, they feature in a number of spice mixes added during cooking or as an accompanying seasoning, such as Indonesian *sambals* (a purée of hot peppers, sometimes with garlic and lemon), Thai curry pastes, or North African harissa. At home, hot peppers—like many other spices—are generally pounded in wooden or stone mortars (facing page, a Mexican stone mortar).

and political resilience remained as strong as ever.

In Szechwan province, hot peppers are not only served as a garnish for noodles: their fieriness crops up everywhere, often in sauces mixed with Szechwan pepper, ginger, and garlic. In the United States, and particularly in Texas, the proximity of Mexico has encouraged dishes with hot peppers, heralding the birth of TexMex cooking. Its masterpiece is the famous chili con carne, the beef stew with beans well seasoned with several types of pepper that ranchers were already enjoying in the nineteenth century. There are many kinds of chili powders in the region, and their generally mild recipes are jealously guarded by their producers.

In the West Indies, chili-pepper delicacies are distinctly hotter: here, in the birthplace of the capsicum, its triumphant world tour comes full circle. The Creole language boasts a long list of poetic names for all the various peppers, for example the thin and extremely tart *z'ozio* (known in English as bird pepper), the long *z'indien*, the round, plump and flaming *bonda a Man Jacques* (which translates as "Madame Jacques buttocks"), the *piment-cerise* (cherrypepper), and the *piment-lampion* (the lanternshaped "Scotch bonnet"), to name only a few. These succulent hot peppers are used to season both blood sausage and acras (vegetable or meat fritters), as well as caris, the chili equivalent of Indian curry, prepared with a spice mix known as "Colombo powder". French Guyana and the French West Indies are also the origin of what is sometimes known as "Cayenne pepper", which in fact consists of several varieties of hot peppers from various places sold as a powder.

To the uninitiated, the use of hot peppers and chilies in the kitchen remains fraught with dangers. The best advice can be summed up in a single word: prudence. It is far better to be disappointed by a meal that is bland than have to throw away a dish that is inedible.

Hot peppers, whether fresh or dried, should be opened before use, seeded and, where possible, cored. This is best done under cold running water in order to avoid covering the fingers in the pepper's stinging alkaloids. A whole undried hot pepper thrown into a simmering saucepan will "heat it up" far less than a chopped one. Nonetheless, if your recipe seems too hot, you can always try to cool it down by adding something starchy–potato, bread, or rice, for example–which, unlike the ineffectual glass of water, will allay the burning sensation in the mouth. When all else fails, if you are invited to eat with Tamil or Szechwan hosts, just try to keep smiling…

Everyday Hungarian paprika (facing page) is the polar opposite of those fierce and fiery chilies (above) that are ground into what is sometimes known as Cayenne pepper. Slightly sweet yet sour, the milder varieties of paprika are indispensable in goulash, and can be used to season other dishes. French chef Paul Bocuse uses it to lend a blush to his airy salmon mousse, while Alain Senderens recommends it for an impeccably weight-conscious cooked red cabbage salad. Paprika also exists in spicier versions, as described by the French writer and diplomat Paul Morand in *Ouvert la nuit*: "The dense heat was forgotten in the fire of dishes cooked with a paprika that drilled through the cheeks and could only be quenched with white wine from Pressburg." Following double page spread: in Hungary, dried peppers are finely powdered to make paprika.

Four spices in one :
Jamaican allspice

This odd-looking crinkly brown berry, scarcely larger than a peppercorn, looks very much like peppercorn, and some call it "Jamaica pepper" because it grew chiefly on that island. But, as its flavor is suggestive of other spices, in English it is known as allspice, while in French it is known as "four spices", after a traditional mix for terrines and stews whose flavor it recalls. Most shops today call it allspice; as for the Jamaicans, they call it *pimento*.

BOUQUETS OF ALLSPICE
A walk on the heights of the Blue Mountains, where the best coffee in the world grows, amid the jasmine-like scent of coffee flowers, brings home to the visitor the fact that Jamaica is one of the most fragrant islands in the world. Walking back down the hillside above the seashore, you suddenly become aware of a strong perfume of cloves. Cloves in Jamaica? From a little farther off comes the sound of reggae. As you approach, the fragrance of cloves, now mingled with a cinnamon sweetness and a more floral note, becomes heavier still. All of a sudden you find yourself in the middle of a plantation of magnificent smooth-trunked trees, their impressive foliage dotted with little white flowers. Music blares from a transistor radio. Perched high up in the trees, young pickers nip off the tips of branches, hung with bunches of green berries resembling peas, and let them plummet to the ground. A little way off, a group of women and children sit at the foot of a tree behind a pile of branches from which, with tremendous care, they remove the green berries—the allspice—

before placing them in a large canvas bag. Like the exquisitely scented flowers, the berries too give off a pungent fragrance of clove that becomes stronger if you squeeze them between your fingers. The allspice is stored in sacks for a few days to "sweat" a bit, before being sun-dried on broad platforms for five to ten days. Raked over constantly, the berries turn brown in color and lose half their weight. After sifting to remove debris, the "pimento" is ready for sale.

A HEAVENLY BOUQUET
If you shake a grain of allspice, especially a large one, you can hear the two seeds—like two miniature coffee beans—rattling inside. When the time comes to grind or pound the berry (at the very last moment if possible), the rather bland seeds soften the delicious piquancy of the outside to produce a subtle combination of flavors: first comes clove, followed by peppercorn, and finally a dash of cinnamon and nutmeg. The intensity of these last two flavors depends on the harvest and country of origin: some allspice comes from Mexico and others from Central American countries.

Because it combines the four cardinal spices instead of being itself a fifth, the humble allspice has had to put up with numerous soubriquets in other languages. In one respect at least it remains unvanquished: despite innumerable attempts, no one has ever succeeded in uprooting it from its cherished Americas. Plants have been exported to India, Sri Lanka, Malaysia and even Australia. The trees grow, the flowers fill the air with their

Jamaican allspice (facing page) is common in Great Britain and northern Europe, where its strong flavor—a subtle combination of cloves, pepper, cinnamon, and nutmeg—is greatly appreciated, though it remains strangely neglected in countries like France. Once ground (it helps to crush it a little first as the berry is really too large for most pepper mills), it boasts a generous and rich flavor that complements all dishes generally seasoned with pepper. The Arawak Indians of Xamayca (Jamaica) were its earliest connoisseurs, using it in quantities to perfume the smoke with which they cured their meat. The tradition is maintained on the island in the form of the highly-spiced chargrilled jerk pork.

sugar and juniper, allspice also seasons the traditional Irish spiced beef flap and numerous desserts, puddings and biscuits. It is highly prized too in Scandinavia, where it is used to season herring and fish marinades, meat balls, liver pâté, and a strangely gelatinous dried cod dish, steeped in water for forty-eight hours before being coated with a white sauce seasoned with allspice. In Germany, it complements cold meats and fish. In France it has made an appearance, with characteristically subtle discretion, in a spicy mix known as "five berries" (or "five peppers"), where it accompanies "red peppercorns" and the three "true" peppercorns. It also appears in liqueurs originating from the monastic foundations of Benedictine and Chartreuse.

In the French Antilles—on Guadaloupe and Martinique—allspice enjoys a place in every kitchen flavoring fish, shellfish and blood sausages alike. But in its birthplace, Jamaica, the easy-going "pimento" really comes into its own. A spice of the people, it accompanies everyday dishes such as chicken in sauce, or more festive ones such fish sautéed in spices—in which hot chili peppers also make an appearance—and above all jerk pork, a dish that really constitutes an ode to allspice. Leaves from the allspice tree are laid over pork that has been macerated in spices (including allspice, of course, but also cinnamon and chili), which is then broiled in the open air over embers from branches of the same tree. The heady, smoky fragrance that rises from the fire—drifting up into the blue sky on the sea breeze—seems to carry you off to paradise.

heavy scent, but mysteriously no fruit appears. Hence allspice remains the only major spice confined to a single continent.

Imported to Europe by the English, its versatile flavor has succeeded in permeating the kitchens of Europe—with the notable and highly enigmatic exception of southern Europe, France included. It is commonly used in Great Britain and Ireland. As Elizabeth David notes in her *Spices, Salt and Condiments in the English Kitchen*: "The main use of allspice in English cooking is to give an aromatic scent to marinades and pickling mixtures for soused herring, salt beef, pickled pork and the like." In association with cane

In France, because of its combination of the four flavors its evokes, Jamaican allspice is sometimes called "quatre épices" or "four spices", a name which is always liable to lead to confusion with the ground mix of spices traditionally used in French cuisine, known for centuries by the same name. Used to flavor terrines, stews and thick soups, the authentic French "four spice" mix comprises black pepper, nutmeg, clove and ginger.

Pepper,
the fiery berry

Long ago, in his *Natural History*, the great naturalist Pliny expressed his surprise in the face of his generation's extraordinary infatuation with pepper. "It is astonishing that its use has met with such favor. In other foods, it is their sweetness that enchants us, or else it is their appearance that beguiles; but, as for pepper, neither its fruit nor its berry has anything to recommend it. To think that it is just for its bitterness that people like it, and that they go to India in search for it." He was right: why such a craze for pepper? Does it come down to mere patrician snobbery? History demonstrates that it does not. Our taste buds crave soft, sensual caresses, but they also need regular contacts of a stronger, more fiery nature. Thus the two sensations require and complement one another: without pepper, without chili, our gastronomic pleasure would not be complete.

HARVESTING PEPPER

For centuries little has changed in the cultivation of pepper on the southwest coast of India, known as the Malabar or the Pepper Coast. The exception—in response to high global demand—is a degree of rationalization in the production process. In India, as in Brazil, Indonesia and Malaysia, you find the same wooden stakes—or other species of tree—planted in long lines in order to support the trailing fronds of *Piper nigram*, which twine around them like dense ivy. Trees such as coconut palms, jack, or other exotic tropical species are used, their sparse canopies of leaves allowing the sun to filter through and ripen the little bunches of fruit.

Thus in Kerala, first thing in the morning, pickers arrive in the pepper groves, a wicker basket slung over their shoulders. Each is then

Pepper grows in long, thin bunches on a creeper (above, pepper plants in 1930s Borneo in the Malaysian state of Sarawak, producer of some of the world's finest pepper; a bunch of pepper ready for picking). Though pepper is our most common spice, there are nevertheless some unusual and delicious uses for it. Chef Roger Vergé, for instance, in his book *Les fruits de mon moulin*, recommends cooking fruit in wine with a few grains of black peppercorn (tied up in a muslin sachet), as well as serving pepper with strawberries, pineapple, and melon.

handed a long bamboo ladder, for the creeper can climb as high as thirty-five feet around a coconut trunk.

In the production of black pepper, the bunches of little corns are detached by hand when still green and not quite ripe. These bunches are then transported to the factory and stripped. The corns are put out to dry in the sun for several days on the ground, where they are aired constantly with large rakes to avoid any fermentation. The green corn gradually shrivels, puckers, and adopts its final color. It is then winnowed for a long time to separate any impurities, before being graded. Corns destined to make white pepper are harvested only when fully ripe and deep red in color. Fully mature, the berry's fragile external sheath can easily be removed by hand, after first being fermented for a time in salt water. The creamy white seed that then emerges from beneath the outer pulp is quickly dried and carefully sorted. It is this extra handling that makes it more expensive than black pepper.

A PALETTE OF PEPPERS

White pepper and black pepper thus come from the same fruit, one removed from the pulp, the other not. Their differences do not lie solely in their color and price, however. Most of the piperine, the pungent substance contained in pepper, is found in the "skin" around the seed, whereas the aroma of its essential oils is contained within the seed itself. This explains why white pepper is less fiery but richer in flavor than black.

Both sorts were already known to the Ancients. The Romans, however, appreciated a third pepper of Indian origin, *Piper longum*, which continued to be used in the Middle Ages and is enjoying a healthy revival today. The corns are far smaller in size, grouped into a spike three-quarters of an inch long that acquires its light brown color when it is sun-dried. This pepper is generally sold as a spike and ground as needed. Hot as black peppercorn, its slightly acidic and sweet flavor is distinctive and well suited to seasoning game, for example. It is also excellent in salad dressings and gives good body to any meat sauce.

Along with *Piper longum*, the *cubeb*–or "tailed pepper"–is another spice that was celebrated in the Middle Ages and is now coming to the fore again. *Piper cubeba*, grown primarily on Sri Lanka and in Indonesia, yields small fruits of a size and appearance similar to black pepper, but with a unusual stalk. Because its flavor is also very close to that of black pepper, though slightly more bitter and aromatic, it can be used in place of normal pepper. Olivier Rœllinger, for example, sprinkles it over stewed calves' liver served with a fruit chutney. The last of these medieval "peppers" to find grace in today's kitchens is a spice known since the Middle Ages as "grains of paradise", sometimes called "Guinea pepper". Its lightly acidic yet "explosive" seeds come from the fruit–used also in voodoo rituals–of a common African plant, *Aframomum melegueta*. Less fragrant than pepper proper, "grains of paradise" are rarely used in the West. They are found in many different African dishes, however, and are an ingredient in the famous Moroccan spice mix, *ras el-hanout*.

The appearance of "fagara" in stores of Western spice merchants is one of the best things to happen in the recent history of spices. Originally from the Szechwan province in China, it may also be encountered as Szechwan pepper. For pepper lovers, the dried seeds of *Zanthoxylum piperitum*, which when ripe split in two, offer a potent flavor–as well as a lovely rose color–mingling floral, lemon, and menthol notes, accompanied by a striking acrid quality.

The climbing shrub known as the pepper provides, as well as the untreated fruit, green pepper, aromatic black pepper and pungent white (facing page). The former is simply the dried fruit, while the latter has had the outer pulp removed. They can be mixed together to create a fine crushed pepper seasoning, mignonette, used for steak *au poivre*. Following double page spread: "Muntok" pepper being loaded at the beginning of the twentieth century: one of the best Indonesian "vintages", this is also available as white pepper.

On the plantations (above, in Kerala India) one of the principal tasks is the cleaning and sorting of the peppercorns. For trader and customer alike, the best pepper can be recognized by its regular shape and the absence of debris or defective corns. From the same *Piper* family as everyday pepper, Indian long pepper (facing page) grows in minuscule spikes that are ground or pounded. Originally from southern Asia, it was already highly prized in ancient Rome, where it was the most expensive of the peppers, as Pliny observed in his *Natural History*: "The long pepper sells at fifteen denarii a pound, the white at seven, the black at four." As pungent as black pepper, but slightly acidic and sweet, it makes an interesting variation on the pepper theme, especially for tangy recipes such as marinades and salads. Prevalent until the Middle Ages, it is now to be found in only the very best grocery stores.

Both aroma and flavor are enhanced even further by gently roasting it in a skillet and crushed it quickly in a mortar and pestle before use. *Fagara* is the most essential spice in Szechwan cuisine, where it used in considerable quantities: Peking duck would be incomplete without it, as would any recipe calling for "five spice powder". Sottha Khunn, a disciple of Alain Sederens who is chef at New York's "Cirque", enjoys great success with a remarkable dish of cod baked with Szechwan pepper. Ken Hom, one of the foremost authorities on Chinese cuisine, recommends a few pinches on pan-fried foie gras.

Seemingly infinite in its variations and fascinating in its history, the queen of all the spices never fails to spark the imagination of gourmets. Historians of the pleasures of eating are equally delighted when they can identify a true innovation, as in the case of green pepper. Green peppercorns are simply the undried berries of black pepper, picked as a cluster on the bush and sold in this form, complete with stalk, in the markets of India. Here and in Thailand too, people have always appreciated the delicately fruity taste of fresh pepper, which they can add to many dishes. But the extraordinary vogue recently enjoyed by green pepper, first in France and then in the rest of the world, dates only from the 1960s. The catalyst in this pepper revolution was Claude Terrail, chef at the prestigious Tour d'Argent restaurant in Paris. In the early 1960s he brought back a few bunches of green pepper from a voyage to Santo Domingo and used it to add a dash of sunshine to his stuffing for duckling. Shortly afterwards, the great purveyor of fine foods, Paul Corcellet was to launch a vogue for an exquisite green pepper mustard. Green pepper is now sold in a number of forms: as a conserve or in brine, deep-frozen or freeze-dried.

Some fifteen years after Terrail's journey to Santo Domingo, one of the most perspicacious

of all French spice traders, Bernard Broquère, undertook a similar voyage of discovery to Réunion. The handsome sign of his shop, "Au Comptoir colonial" on Rue Lepic in the Montmartre district of Paris can be seen everywhere on labels of bottles containing his spices of the utmost quality. Strolling one day on the heights of Réunion, he came upon a bush with pink flowers and fruits which, he discovered, was believed by the local people to be so toxic that not only did they never consume the fruits—which resembled pink peppercorns—but they also avoided even touching it.

Disregarding their warnings, Bernard Broquère tried a seed. It was like pepper but was deliciously fruity, less piquant and slightly

Used since earliest times in China, the lovely rose-colored berry of *fagara*, known ground as Szechwan pepper (facing page, top), possesses the most astonishing flavor possible to imagine. Its sharp lemony notes, piquant and lingering, have earned it the favor of many distinguished chefs. Chen, one of the great Chinese chefs in Paris, uses it to flavor his sautéed frog's legs, while at Michel Rostang's restaurant, Stéphane Hottlet has devised an extraordinary sorbet to accompany an apricot pastry *croustillant* with almond sauce. Another wonderful though little-known—or rather forgotten—pepper is the warm and slightly sour *cubeb* (above) adopted by Olivier Rœllinger, which is pounded in a mortar before being sprinkled on meat or vegetable dishes.

(pepper should also be added at a late stage of cooking, as prolonged cooking kills its taste). Peppercorns can be stored almost indefinitely, whereas ready-ground pepper loses its flavor in a few days. The so-called "gray pepper"—always sold ready-ground as it does not exist in seed form—is simply a milled mix of debris and corns of indifferent quality. A much better solution is to make your own mixture, which will be more or less gray in color, by crushing white or black pepper. This crushed pepper seasoning is good with oysters, and can be used in the sauce for steak *au poivre* (for which you can also use pepper milled in a specially designed, coarse-grinding mill). Never forget, either, that the finest peppercorns greatly enhance the flavor of fresh fruit—in particular strawberries, pineapple, and figs. Finally, to achieve more subtle variations of flavor, do not be afraid to blend different kinds of pepper.

sweet. He returned to France bearing a small sachet of seeds which proved under analysis to be the fruits of the completely innocuous *Schinus terebenthifolius*. Bernard Broquère decided to return to Réunion. There, with the greatest difficulty, he hired three pickers who would only work if well protected by gloves. He finally succeeded in bringing back to France around twenty five pounds of the fruit, which he christened "pink pepper". A newspaper article and a television program launched the delectable little seeds in France, and they have since been delighting cooks around the world. In France, where regulations allow only members of the genus *Piper* to be called "pepper", they are now known as *"baies roses"* in French, or "pink berries", while in the English-speaking world they are known as "pink peppercorns". Whether pepper is green, pink, black, or white, it is a cast-iron rule that it should be purchased loose and milled just before use

The blazing colors of the different peppers give as much pleasure to the eye as their flavors do to the taste buds. Green pepper (top), the freshest and fruitiest of the peppers, is splendid with *magret de canard*, veal *filet mignon* or scallops. The colorful and now classic "five berries" or "five peppers" (above) graces many dishes, both savory as sweet. "Pink peppercorns", the sweetest of the non-*Piper* peppers (facing page, in a magnificent Indian spice box), suit fish terrines, salads, and poultry dishes, their flavor being so mild that they can be added whole. The fiery "grains of paradise"(following double-page spread), are the oldest of the false peppers, frequently used as a seasoning in Africa where it is grown.

Saffron,
the flower of spices

Imagine a flower that blooms at night, its mauve petals pushing through the soil before dawn like a small flame to open with the early-morning dew. The nocturnal magic of *Crocus sativus*, today known as saffron (Arabic *zaha-faran*, from *asfar*, yellow), was the inspiration for one of the thousands of Asian legends surrounding Alexander the Great. Having reached Kashmir in the autumn of 327 BC, the conquering general gave orders for his army to pitch camp in an arid valley. They awoke next morning to find the entire valley carpeted with blue and mauve flowers, which had even pushed up beneath their tents and chariots. Taking this as a bad omen, Alexander decided to go no farther but to retrace his steps. Thus he ended his conquest of the world.

GARDENS OF MAUVE AND YELLOW
The color for which saffron is celebrated throughout the world is the color of dawn, as hymned by Homer in the *Iliad* as he described "dawn with its saffron veil". Between first light and daybreak, the sky turns brilliant yellow, shimmering gold and orange: this is the saffron yellow that has been used to dye fabrics and to color food for five thousand years, derived from the flower's three red stigmas.

Removed and dried, five of these filaments, weighing a hundredth of a gram (around a seventh of a grain), can infuse a pint and a half of water with a vivid yellow color—or lend

a divine aroma. This is the magic of saffron.

The Romans and Phoenicians spread their taste for saffron throughout Europe. At that time, the flower grew principally in Mesopotamia, Persia, and Kashmir. From the eighth century, the Arabs extended its cultivation to Spain, a country which still today provides some of the world's best saffron. Gradually, in the years following the Crusades, saffron's mauve flowers spread into France, to the Loire area and especially into the Gâtinais (thirty miles south of Paris), where its cultivation, once well-established before the 1880s, is slowly beginning to re-emerge on a small scale. Saffron was also cultivated in Germany from the eleventh century, and three centuries later in England, particularly around the small village of Chypping Walden, in Essex, rechristened Saffron Walden in 1514 by Royal Charter of Henry VIII.

The deadliest enemy of saffron is hard frost, responsible for the destruction of saffron fields in the Gâtinais following the two arctic winters of 1880 and 1881. The flower, in fact, is not difficult to cultivate and will grow virtually anywhere, though with a preference for chalky soils, hot dry summers, cold winters, and rainy springs. Today, the beautiful mauve-striped expanses of saffron fields can be found in fifteen countries and on every continent.

For thousands of years, saffron–the only spice derived from a flower in full bloom–has yielded a legendary aroma, its mystique enhanced by the lovely colors of the flowers. Their three downy orange stamens and, above all, the pure deep red of their three precious long stigmas, are delicately silhouetted against the blue-mauve of the fine silky petals (above). Infinite patience is required for the task of removing the stigmas (facing page), the 'peelers' or *mondadoras* of Spain (whence the most sought-after saffron comes) enjoying a reputation second to none. Every year at Consuegra in Castille, the end of the harvest (following double page spread, men picking saffron flowers) is celebrated with a splendid fiesta in honour of the *rosa del azafran*.

The great saffron-producing countries are just four in number: Iran and Spain (whose produce is marketed in most countries), followed by India, which consumes the majority of its Kashmiri production, and lastly, with a smaller yield, Greece. The economics of the spice–as well as the passion and patient industry of the saffron farmer–can be gauged from the following statistic: it takes no fewer than one hundred and fifty thousand flowers to produce two and a quarter pounds of dry saffron.

What is more, the fragile flowers can only be picked and stripped by hand. This is the simple reason why world production never rises much above a hundred tons, and why saffron is by far the most expensive and most precious spice of all. In all the world's saffron fields, the tasks are much the same.

In early September in central Spain, on the vast plain of La Mancha–where the pretty windmills against which Don Quixote lowered his lance still turn–women known *roseras* bend double to pick the "saffron roses" from only an inch or so above the ground. In this region, the saffron plantations–*celaminas*–are rarely larger than an eighth of an acre. The stooping pickers move slowly along a line of mauve, using both hands to nip off the stalks at the base of the petals, between thumbnail and index finger. Once they have a dozen or so flowers in the palm of their hand, they stand up and drop them into a wicker basket. The harvest takes place every morning for three months, and every day, the picked flowers are carried off to the farm where the *monda*–the removal of the three stigmas that carry the saffron–takes place. Women of every generation sit around the large kitchen table, amid the delicately fruity and ever more intense aroma of the petals, which fall to the floor like rain. By nightfall, each one of them will have stripped–with nimble and now blue fingers–around ten thousand flowers. For hours, they dislodge the petals from each flower, and with a fingernail slice through the style that forms a base holding all three red filaments.

Jean-Marie Thiercelin, one of the few world experts on saffron, and last in a long line of valuers and traders from the Gâtinais, may now be found in his small store near the Opéra in Paris. When asked why La Mancha saffron is among the best in the world, it is the *monda* that he mentions first. On the farms of La Mancha, the *mondadoras* cut the style as close as possible to the stigmas, which alone contain all the fragrance of saffron. The high quality of *Mancha* also derives from the final drying process, during which the filaments lose four-fifths of their weight.

In Asian countries, they are gathered into tiny bunches and slowly dried. In La Mancha, they are placed in screens over a brazier and thus dried cleanly, quickly, and thoroughly. From the kitchens of La Mancha, there emanates quite a different fragrance, a bouquet of earth, mushrooms, and smoke, with notes of licorice, sandalwood, and peppercorns: a divinely complex aroma destined to leave in the mouth a delicate hint of bitterness that only saffron can yield.

Saffron sold by the finest retailers has the date of its harvest printed on the packaging, since only fresh saffron (facing page) offers its full richness and subtlety. Its slightly fruity and woody bitterness may be used to enhance risotto, paella, Swedish rolls, and English cakes. It is also splendid in bouillabaisse, described by the English novelist and food-lover John Lanchester in his highly entertaining book *The Debt to Pleasure* as "a combination of luxuriousness and practicality, of romance and realism... characteristic of the Marseillais themselves". Evoked by Marcel Pagnol in *Les temps des amours*, "pilaf of mussels with rice is marvelously flavored with saffron". Above, a clutch of attractive old saffron boxes.

THE ART OF SAFFRON

Pliny warned first-century saffron-lovers in the twenty-first book of his *Natural History*: "Nothing is so frequently counterfeited." Scarce and costly, saffron has always been subject to wretched imitations and shameful mistreatment. Fraud chiefly affects powdered saffron. The most frequent and least offensive substitute is turmeric (also known as curcuma and occasionally "Indian saffron"), or the little flowers, more or less crushed, of a dye plant known as safflower (*Carthamus tinctoris*, also known as "bastard saffron"). The majority of the "saffrons" sold loose as powder or filaments in the souks of the Middle East are safflower, while those in powder form in North Africa, on the Mascarenes, or in India, tend to be turmeric–this fact the vendors freely acknowledge. The most recent form of adulteration, which is particularly pernicious as it is so difficult to detect, consists of mixing dyed styles in with the stigmas.

How can you tell true saffron from false without tasting or smelling it? For a start, saffron should be purchased not as a powder but as filaments, since in this form any fraud can generally be detected with the naked eye. A true saffron filament is three-quarters of an inch to an inch and a quarter long and oxblood red in color, becoming slightly lighter at the base towards the remnants of the style. At the other extremity, it opens out like a trumpet with a somewhat jagged-edged horn.

Before use, the filaments should be carefully broken in pieces. If it is not too fresh, it should be sufficient simply to crumble it between the fingers. If it is from a fresh crop (as it ideally should be), on the other hand, then the required amount should first be heated for a minute in a little frying-pan or in the oven, before crumbling the dried filaments between the fingers as before, or pounding them in a little mortar. It is also possible to leave some whole or crumbled filaments to infuse for a time in hot water (or in any non-fatty liquid included in your recipe), before adding the infusion to the dish during cooking.

If necessary, the infusion can later be frozen in an ice-tray, as recommended by the saffron connoisseur John Humphries in his excellent book published in 1996, *The Essential Saffron Companion*. If you find you need some at the last minute, you can then simply melt one or two ice-cubes.

In order to retain its flavor, saffron should be added at the very end of cooking. Few recipes indicate the exact amount of saffron to be added, most being content with vague terms such as "a pinch" or "a little". In such cases, it is best not to use more than a tenth of a gram (one and a half grains), that is around forty stigmas. This is generally enough for a medium-spiced recipe for four to six people–throwing a new slant on the notion of saffron as an expensive luxury!

Saffron endows dishes with an inimitable and slightly bitter flavor of mushrooms, at

The most costly spice of all the spices, saffron is also the most often imitated and counterfeited. In the quest to imitate its lovely color, everything has been tried, including brick dust! What matters is that the imitation should not be passed off as the real thing. In the ingredients listed on the label of this delicious picalilli (above)–a condiment based on vegetables in a vinegar, sugar, and ginger sauce that the British adore–the makers have made no attempt to conceal that its saffron-like color derives from the addition of turmeric.

once woody and fruity, which is the distinguishing feature of a number of gastronomic classics, from the authentic paella of Valencia to bouillabaisse from Marseille. But it is perhaps the deliciously creamy risotto *alla milanese* (known by Italian purists as "risotto with saffron", as the *milanese* was originally white, with no saffron) that best brings out its rich aroma. Risotto with saffron—one of the traditional banquet dishes of medieval Flanders and Lombardy, unified under Emperor Charles V—was valued for more than just its taste: rice, a fertility symbol, is here associated with saffron, itself a symbol of the sun and its health-giving rays. In Flanders and Lombardy, therefore, and from the Middle Ages onwards, risotto with saffron was standard fare for wedding feasts, as depicted in the dish carried in by two servants in Bruegel the Elder's famous *Wedding Banquet*. Besides immemorial recipes such as these, there are also less

well-known traditional saffron dishes, such as gloriously smooth Cornish saffron cakes or numerous Moroccan tajines. Saffron also has its moment of glory in Sweden, thanks to the rolls and cakes baked with it which all true Swedes feast upon at dawn on St Lucy's Day, December 13. According to tradition, at five o'clock in the morning, a young girl dressed all in white and crowned with lighted candles should enter her parents' or the guests' bedroom to serve these saffron delicacies with tea or coffee. Nobel prizewinners, in Stockholm that day for the prestigious prizewinning ceremony, sometimes find themselves at the receiving end of this custom as they slumber peacefully in their hotel rooms—without always having been warned in advance!

Saffron also boasts certain properties that seem so magical that they remain inexplicable: even in practically infinitesimal doses it can be used to temper or accentuate other flavors. Thus the remarkable chocolate-maker Robert Linxe relates how, while trying to create a chocolate with basil—the "Flamenco"—and being disappointed with the metallic taste the herb gave his *crème ganache*, he first added rosemary, then cardamom and jasmine, before finally, after a full year of trial and error, trying a soupçon of saffron. It proved the only flavor capable of marrying chocolate with basil in a manner that flattered both. The most extraordinary thing, however, was that to perform the miracle, a mere six filaments, that is no more than a hundredth of a gram (seventh of a grain) were sufficient for thirteen pounds of ice cream. One last and particularly beguiling idea: a thin slice of lightly toasted bread with saffron is incomparable—especially when it accompanies, with due solemnity, a wafer-thin slice of foie gras.

Passing off the seed of the annato tree (*Bixa orellana*, a strong dye with no particular flavor) as saffron is a criminal offense. Many cheeses contain annato (Edam and Cheddar, for example), as do traditional dishes from the West Indies. Olivier Rœllinger also uses it to lend a red blush to the sophisticated infusion in which he cooks his unforgettable "Little lobsters with spice islands' dressing", based on annato oil, a bouquet of spices and crab *fumet*.

In his *Travels*, Marco Polo reported that turmeric—a fine rhizome of the ginger family—was a "fruit resembling saffron". Peppery and slightly sour, turmeric—also known as "Indian saffron" or curcuma—is generally used fresh (above) or as a powder (facing page) to color Indian curries or the *caris* of the French West Indies. Widespread in Asia, it replaces saffron as a dyestuff and is also supposed to relieve colds. In India its luminous color is meant to bring luck: a dot is placed on the foreheads of newborn infants and it is rubbed over the hems of wedding saris.

Vanilla,
the sweet orchid

On the Indian Ocean island of Réunion, the memory of Edmond Albius is venerated to this day, for it was this young black slave who in 1841 is said to have discovered the process of artificially pollinating the vanilla plant. This chance discovery was re-created by Georges Limbour in his novel *Les Vanilliers* (1938). Among the orchid blooms, after deflowering the young Jeannette, Edmond, amusing himself by twanging the young girl's comb, breaks one of its teeth. This gives him an idea: "Look… Let's stick it in the flower". As he carefully edged the tooth in among the petals, Jeannette cries: "Oh! now she too is a woman! … Perhaps she'll become very beautiful and have children."

AN EXTRAORDINARY ALCHEMIC EVENT

Only an erotic metaphor, indeed, can do justice to the entrancing nature of the orchid we know as vanilla (from the Spanish *vainilla*, meaning literally "little sheath"), and more particularly to its sweet scent, so heady that in sufficient quantities it can prove intoxicating. The conquistador Hernan Cortés, who reached Mexico in 1520, was one of the first Westerners to inhale the exquisite fragrance which the inhabitants extracted from the fruit of a wild orchid unknown in the Old World. Known as *tlilxochili* to the Aztecs, it was an ingredient of the drink to which Emperor Montezuma and his court were so partial, *tchocolatl*: our chocolate, in which the Spanish were soon to become the unrivaled specialists in Europe. Vanilla plants were soon being imported and cosseted lovingly in a few botanic gardens. In the warm, damp atmosphere of a greenhouse,

the orchid grew well enough, producing a generous spread of ephemeral blooms, but it steadfastly refused to produce its fruit, the long pods fermented by the Aztecs to distill their flavor. For many years, this failure to bear fruit remained a mystery. After observing vanilla plants in Mexico, scientists at last understood that the hermaphrodite orchid was unable to fertilize itself; a sort of hymen—a lamella formed by one of the lobes of the stigma—prevented the pollen from penetrating the flower. Pollination could only be carried out by small bees or hummingbirds, which while gathering the nectar would pierce the lamella.

It seems that the first botanist to solve the problem was one Neumann who, ten years before Edmond Albius, had the idea of puncturing the lobe with a slender probe. The experiment, carried out in the greenhouses of the Jardin des Plantes in Paris, was an unqualified success. Today, artificial pollination is standard in practically all regions where vanilla grows, in Madagascar or Réunion, Mexico or Tahiti. As is often the case with such meticulous processes, the task is carried out exclusively by women, known on the island of Réunion as *marieuses*, or "matchmakers". From September to December, on the windy, rainy east coast, the vanilla groves are invaded by groups of these diligent women, the most skilled of whom can pollinate up to a thousand white orchids per day, using only a splinter from a lemon tree or bamboo. Vanilla is a closely-guarded secret here, protected not only from theft but also from hurricanes, planted in shady undergrowth at the foot of tropical trees—casuarina or vacoas—or trained up stakes

In Mexico, where the Aztecs used it to flavor chocolate, the hermaphrodite vanilla plant was pollinated by bees or the long bills of small birds. Not until the first half of the nineteenth century was this phenomenon fully understood, whereupon it was imitated artificially by hand using some sort of thorn. The French then started to plant vanilla groves on the Mascarenes and the West Indies, with the English following suit in India, and the Dutch in Indonesia. The exceptionally dexterous women who carry out this work can pollinate up to a thousand vanilla flowers a day (facing page, Madagascar, the world's largest producer). The operation requires as much rapidity as skill, since the flowers last only a day. The fruits—or "pods"—are picked nine months later.

Once picked, the fresh vanilla pods (facing page) embark on a treatment process that stretches over several months (above, one of the stages, drying out on frames). Once processing is complete the vanilla may well undergo yet further transformations. In the eighteenth century, already popular throughout the world (in the United States, President Thomas Jefferson had a passion for it), vanilla appeared in the form of liqueurs and ointments with supposedly aphrodisiac properties (above, insert, a French nineteenth-century ointment tin).

*A*fter processing, the elastic, oily vanilla pods, now well-defined with ridges, are ready to yield up their extraordinary aroma. In many countries this is the favorite flavoring of all, preferred even to strawberry and chocolate. To preserve their flavor during shipping, the pods are bound into little bundles, wrapped in greaseproof paper and packed into metal boxes (above). Occasionally they are matured, exuding crystals of vanillin, their principal aromatic ingredient, which impart a truly exceptional quality to these "frosted pods" (facing page).

in small clearings deep in the sugar cane plantations. Vanilla is a creeper which likes to twine around a tree, flourishing in the heat and damp shade.

The fruits begin to appear around a month after pollination. These are the pods that the world is waiting for, but they have yet to ripen for another seven or eight months. The pods resemble oversized green beans that slowly turn yellow and can be up to ten inches long. The first harvest begins around June, as soon as the pods have taken on a particular shade of yellow, known on Réunion as "canary tail". Too early, and the pod will be short on flavor; too late, and it will be open and useless.

At this point, an extraordinary alchemic process starts to turn this long, odorless, yellowish fruit into a sublime aromatic concentrate. It might be assumed that this would simply be the equivalent of the fermentation practised by the Aztecs, who laid the pods out in the sun before burying them under straw, breaking them up, and spreading them with oil. In fact, a host of other processes have been developed in order to extract still more flavor. On Réunion, however, where they produce small quantities of one of the best "Bourbon vanillas", fermentation is carried out according to principles that are as complex and mysterious as they are unchanging. In the four firms that share the island's yearly yield of six tons of vanilla, the process starts with blanching the pods—placed in large wicker baskets—in a tank

of water at 60° C (125° F) for three minutes to halt vegetative reproduction. They are then left to sweat in wool-padded crates for twelve hours or so. By now slightly wrinkly, they are already starting to take on their ultimate chocolate-brown color.

After tanking, the pods are dried alternately on racks and in the oven for a week, before being placed in the sun a few hours a day for a further week. It is in the next eight months—during which the pods are closeted away in greaseproof-paper lined crates to secrete their vanillin—that their extraordinary and increasingly marked flavor develops. The pods then emerge in all their glory—almost black, elastic, oily, shiny, and with a heavy scent quite distinct from any that of other fruit. If they were left to age in their crates for a further one or two years, their bottom end would gradually become coated in a sort of pale-yellow spangled "frosting": these are vanillin crystals exuding from the fruit.

Almost a year after being harvested, the vanilla pod is at last ready for the kitchen. Before this, though, the pods are carefully sorted and the split or broken ones packed off to other plants, where they are either powdered or, after maceration in alcohol, transformed into liquid vanilla extract. The finer whole ones are graded by size (the longer ones being the more expensive), tied into batches, then, after a month under observation, shipped off to the distributors who package them as they wish.

Traditionally, vanilla is used for flavoring chocolate, egg custard, cream cakes, fruit desserts, and ice cream. But, as chefs are increasingly aware, its supremely sweet mildness can add a subtly delicious note to white meat and fish or seafood, such as salmon or lobster. Alain Passard, chef at L'Arpège in Paris, recommends it for adding zest to a tomato salad with olive oil and raspberry dressing: score half a pod and macerate it in the salad oil, then the sprinkle the tomato rounds with basil and mint and serve them with toast. (Above: another stage of the treatment process: tanking in hot water.)

THE DELIGHTS OF AUTHENTICITY

Traditional "Bourbon vanilla" is the *Vanilla planifolia*, with which most people would be quite content; but there also exists *Vanilla tahitensis*, from Tahiti, with bulkier pods, which has seduced the most sophisticated gourmet cooks and perfumers with its higher levels of piperonal (an aromatic compound reminiscent of the heliotrope that perfumers call "heliotropin"). This imparts a slightly aniseed-like and still more heady aroma to the vanilla—as well as commanding a very high price that renders it even scarcer. Certain great chefs-patissiers, such as Pierre Hermé in Paris, are prepared to pay the earth for it.

Vanilla is such an appealing flavor that it is a perennial children's favorite. It is used to flavor a large number of today's desserts, ice creams, yogurts, and baby foods. But this enthusiasm is hardly new, and from the early nineteenth century, chemists have striven to synthesize an aromatic equivalent to vanillin that might fulfill the same demand at lower cost. But synthetic vanilla offers none of the aniseed, acidic or pleasantly licorice overtones, no monsoon rains or sunshine. And none of those highly aromatic little black grains that abound in real pods decorate our main courses and desserts alike with their pretty flecking—the cast-iron guarantee of authenticity. Similarly, since the "frosted" pods, sweeter and more "rounded" in the mouth than the others, are unfortunately rarer that other kinds, lack-lustre imitations have started to

spring up, produced with the aid of synthetic "frosted" vanillin that is sprayed onto the pods. They can be detected, however, by the way the "frost" spreads evenly all the whole length of the pod.

A nobler practice is the use of coumarin—a substance recalling vanilla and honey that is extracted from the tonka bean, the seed of a tropical American tree—used in perfumery and confectionery. In past centuries, it was used to impart its delicate vanilla flavor on certain pipe tobaccos. The tonka bean, recently given a place in the kitchen by a number of top chefs, can be used to flavor desserts, sauces, or vegetable purées.

Cooks have recently discovered the extent to which vanilla can confer a mild depth on meat and fish cooked in sauces, and most especially curries. The pod is sliced through the middle and added to the sauce—or else the black grains alone are used. For desserts, vanilla can be infused beforehand in the milk or cream used in the recipe. Our grandmothers traditionally put vanilla pods in sugar. Once impregnated with the vanilla's exquisite aroma, the sugar could be used for tarts, jams, and stewed fruit. Vanilla also customarily adds an extra dash of brightness to rum, punches, and, as on Mauritius, coffee and tea. Bear in mind, finally, that vanilla improves with age, its flavor becoming stronger over time. After infusing—as long as it has been washed and dried before being stored in an air-tight container—there is nothing to prevent using it a second time. This is just one more of the orchid fruit's little miracles.

All the vanilla on the planet—the one from Tahiti (the scarcest and the most sought-after) and "Bourbon" (from Madagascar, the Comoros, and Réunion)—could never hope to satisfy the demands of the world's perfumers and ice-cream makers. The end of the nineteenth century saw the development of synthetic vanillin. Other ersatz vanillas were also discovered, such as coumarin (which also has notes of honey and freshly mown hay), an extract of the tonka bean (above). In South America and the Caribbean, the grated bean is used to flavor a number of recipes, as well as sauces and mashed potatoes. Today European and American cooks are also finding uses for it; Ghislaine Arabian, at Le Doyen, for instance, adds it to a chocolate tart.

The magic of
blending spices

In the gastronomy of the ancient world and of the spice-mad Middle Ages, spices were almost never used singly but were rather combined in order to obtain a specific flavor. Today as well, no highly-seasoned dish from any of the great cuisines that traditionally use spices–the Middle East, India or the West Indies, for example–is without its own special aromatic mix. The often extremely sophisticated recipes for these blends are closely-guarded secrets, handed down from generation to generation like heirlooms. Here we shall confine ourselves to the most celebrated blends, taking the opportunity along the way to introduce a few more spices.

BLENDS OF THE SOUK

Morocco, with its time-honored culinary tradition, boasts the most mysterious and elaborate spice blend of all, the *ras el-hanout*. In her fine book on Moroccan cooking *Gestes et saveurs du Maroc*, Fatéma Hal, who now runs a restaurant in Paris, lists most of the twenty-seven ingredients that go to make up a genuinely authentic *ras el-hanout*, including spices such as hot pepper, ginger, cinnamon, cumin, saffron, nutmeg, and clove, but also rosebuds, belladonna berries, the fruit of the ash, not forgetting gum arabic, and the bizarre Spanish fly, a dried beetle with a reputation as an aphrodisiac.

From time immemorial, the world's cuisines have been blending spices to create flavors to suit specific dishes. In the fragrant souks of Morocco (facing page), the many spices mixed into a *ras el-hanout* that flavor a tajine await blending. Ginger and saffron can be married in the *m'qualli* sauce for chicken with confit of lemon; sweet pepper and cumin are mixed in the *m'hammer* sauce that seasons tajine of mutton. Mixes ready-made for salad and meat or fish grills can be found on market-stalls (above, Cours Saleya, Nice), in delicatessens or supermarkets, and are now making inroads into Western cuisine.

In Lebanon and Syria, *zahtar* (above, in the compartment to the right), deliciously tart thanks to the addition of sumac (facing page), is based on thyme and toasted sesame seeds (above, three different varieties of sesame: golden, black and white). In Egypt, spice vendors in the souk prepare a mixture for meat containing fennel, bay, clove, nutmeg, ginger, cinnamon, cardamom, and white and black peppers in proportions that remain a secret. For a fish seasoning, they add cumin, coriander seeds, oregano, and thyme. These blends can also comprise some red safflower powder from a little flower whose quality as a dye is similar to that of saffron–under which name it is often passed off.

With its warm, piquant notes, the mixture—the name means literally "head of the spice shop"- enhances the flavors of tajines, such as the divinely sweet *muruziya* based on lamb in honey and raisins, as well as pigeon *pastilla* and even sometimes, in Fez, coffee. *Ras el-hanout* also includes coriander, an aromatic plant which in its fresh form is used in Asian cuisine under the name "Chinese parsley". In Oriental and Indian cooking the seeds give the same delicate flavor as in European recipes such as sauerkraut.

In Lebanon, as in Syria and Iraq, it is the flavor of a heavenly blend known as *zahtar* that delights the palate. This mix of spices, ground rather than milled, can be enjoyed on soft white cheese, but it is preferred as an entrée, served on a plate and used as a dip for bread soaked in olive oil. The main ingredient of *zahtar* is toasted sesame seeds, to which are added thyme, coriander seeds, pounded walnuts, cumin, cinnamon and sumac powder. Sumac comes from a bush of the Mediterranean basin whose fruits, growing in clumps of red berries, are dried into a sour-tasting spice widely used in the Middle East. In the most gourmet country in the region, Syria, the spicy cuisine of Aleppo prefers *beahar*, a blend of peppercorns, cinnamon, nutmeg, cloves, and cardamom, the wonderful fragrance of which hangs heavy over the spice souk in the old town.

THE GREAT ART OF CURRY

In Pakistani, Indian, and Ceylonese cuisine, we encounter a singularly elaborate world of spices. The dishes with sauce that are commonly known as curries and the chargrilled meats baked in the little earthenware ovens termed *tandoor*, together with some teas and a large number of chutneys and desserts, are all prepared with a host of different spice mixes. Those that are known the world over as "curry powder", often sold as inferior ready-mixed packets, are unknown in India. The word itself is not even Indian but English, a bastardization of the term *kari* which, in the Madras region, used to denote a dish of spiced vegetables. Moreover, there is not *one* "curry" in India, but dozens of different mixes known as *masalas*. Finally, to prepare an everyday "lamb curry", not one but *three* various *masalas* are used: the first, fried in the oil in which the meat has already been browned a little, comprises ginger, garlic, and hot pepper; the second, which is left to simmer for at least half an hour, marries cardamom with cassia leaves (something like European bay); the third, added only a few minutes before serving, is the mix most often used in curries towards the end of cooking, *garam masala*. Usually mild in taste and wonderfully fragrant, it lends a characteristic touch to any dish with its harmonious blend of black peppercorn, cumin, cardamom, whole cloves, and cinnamon. There are several varieties of *garam masala*, however, some also incorporating nutmeg, mace, caraway seed, coriander or ginger.

Gastronomic nuances, regional and family traditions and a sure hand all have their part to play. The astonishing subtlety of Indian cooking can be gauged from the fact that certain curries require no fewer than five different masalas: in addition to the three that accompany the various stages of cooking, another is used to marinate the meat and a fifth serves as a condiment at the table. Naturally, each of these mixes—which can themselves combine anything from two to twenty ingredients, for the most part grilled and ground before use— varies according to region. Many mixes and all commercial curry powders include turmeric.

*I*ndian *tikka masala* (facing page) incorporates chili peppers, coriander, cumin, poppy seed, peppercorn, cassia, cloves, ginger, garlic, and salt, and accompanies both meat and fish, which is diced and then cooked in earthenware ovens called *tandoor*. Following double-page spread, a range of spices and mixes (from top to bottom and from left to right): sweet pepper, nutmeg, *tandoori masala*, *garam masala*, hot chili pepper, curry powder, a mix for spice breads, a Mexican mix for *tacos*, *tandoori masala*, eastern blends for *kebabs*, spices for paella and couscous, an Indonesian mix for *satay*, curry powder, five spice powder, ginger, cardamom, spices for a *rouille*, fenugreek, hot pepper, turmeric, and vanilla.

TUMERIC

The turmeric rhizome (also known as "cur-cuma") is a cousin of ginger and is sometimes dubbed "Indian saffron", since its main virtue lies in its qualities as a food dye: it is turmeric that imparts their characteristic yellow color to a large number of curry mixes. The predominant flavor of curry powders as they are known in the West derives from the celery and smoky milled fenugreek, a legume widespread in India—where its fresh leaves are consumed as a vegetable—but which also grows in many other countries. Even before milling, the extremely tough yellow seeds give off a strong aroma of curry. For the Western palate—and for the cook in a hurry—the mix that the nineteenthcentury writer George Sand had prepared for her at her residence in Nohant has much to recommend it: no fenugreek, but, for every 3 1/4 oz of mix, 1 3/4 oz of sweet peppers, 1 1/4 oz of turmeric, 1/5 oz of cloves and white pepper, and 30 grains of nutmeg.

FROM "FIVE SPICE POWDER" TO ALLSPICE

Although Thai supermarkets do sell ready-mixed spice blends, you can hardly do better than purchase a "tailor-made" mix in a village market, prepared by an expert vendor to your own requirements and wrapped in a banana leaf. Generally, these are in fact herb and spice pastes known on the market as "curry paste" and are accompanied by the ever-present prawn paste, *kapi.*

The most common version, which makes a strong seasoning for both meat and vegetable dishes comprises—in addition to a little *kapi* and salt—a mix of hot red peppers, onions, garlic, lemon grass, fresh coriander and coriander seeds, peppercorns, cumin, and the chopped zest of a citrus fruit called *makrut* (reminiscent of lime and grapefruit) as well as pounded galingale. The latter, a hot-tasting rhizome related to ginger but with an aroma more reminiscent of eucalyptus, is commonly found in Far Eastern and Chinese cookery. Before lapsing into oblivion in Europe it was known in medieval French by the pretty name of "garingal". In conjunction with lemon grass, it adds a sharp aftertaste to any piquant mix.

Galingale plays no part, however, in the ancient Chinese blend known as "five spice powder" or "Chinese five spice". Also found in Vietnamese cuisine, this is an indispensable ingredient in seasonings for chicken, duck, and pork spare-ribs. Equal quantities of finely-ground Szechwan pepper, cinnamon, cloves, and fennel seed are mixed together with the pretty little fruits of the plant called, for its taste and shape, star anise—the flavoring ingredient in many aniseed alcohols.

The choice of the number five is not the result of chance, however, but derives from ancient Chinese cosmology, which divides the universe into five elements: wood, metal, water, fire, and earth. Like this ideal concept of the universe where the elements are in harmony, the spices blend perfectly in a mixture of flavors that is at once sweet and peppery, giving off a glowing, fruity aroma. "Five spice powder" is sold in little sachets in Chinatowns all over the world, but nothing beats making it

Once ground, the striped seeds of fennel (facing page) and the magnificent sun-shaped star anise (above) lend a strong aniseed flavor to a Chinese spice mix, "five spice powder", with one of the longest traditions used to accompany meat and poultry. In the West, fresh fennel leaves or its seeds are often used to flavor fish, and in India the spice (called *soonf*) is an ingredient in numerous masalas. Star anise—which yields much the same aroma as anise—is an essential ingredient of the popular French alcoholic cordials, *pastis* and *anisette*, and can also be made into an exquisite mustard ideally suited to fish and salads.

fresh from carefully stored spices, grinding it shortly before serving.

Let us leave to industry such overcomplicated concoctions as the famous Worcestershire sauce, the original recipe for which was brought back to England around 1850 by Sir Marcus Sandy–loyal subject of Her Gracious Majesty and resident of Worcestershire–from Bengal, where he had been governor. Acquaintances of his in the food trade attempted to reproduce the recipe and came up with something reasonably close comprising, as well as anchovies and beef extract, soya bean, hot peppers, cloves, and tamarind. The fruit of this magnificent Asian tree, somewhat resembling weeping willow, is an elongated pod, a sort of oversized brown bean containing seeds enclosed in pulp. It is the latter in the main that gives tamarind its pronounced taste of unripe fruit, at once sweet and very tart. As a

preserve or in dried slices, it makes a lively ingredient in numerous Indian curry sauces and chutneys. In Thailand its sour taste gives added "edge" to a number of soups, whereas in the West Indies it is made into a refreshing drink. Making the most of a wealth of influences, in the French West Indies and on the Mascarenes tastes lean towards a spicy-based cuisine in which the "cari" reigns supreme.

In the Belleville quarter of Paris at the celebrated restaurant-cum-delicatessen "Aux Spécialités antillaises", Indira Wootun, a native of Mauritius, demonstrates the subtle distinctions between "curry" and "cari", between Indian *masala* and West Indian *massalés* (pastes)–or their equivalent on Réunion (in powder)– between *massalé* and "Colombo powder". For an Antilles "cari" the "Colombo powder" mix consists of ginger, cloves, turmeric, coriander, peppercorns, hot peppers, fenugreek, mustard grains, and toasted rice. The Indian population of the French West Indies or of Réunion opt rather for *masala*–there called *massalé*–a less fiery blend comprising aniseed, coriander, saffron, chives, onion, peppercorns and cloves, but no turmeric. On these islands where different peoples come into contact and often intermingle, the various cooking styles differ only in details, to be further obscured by the personal flair of individual cooks. Thus for strongly flavored fish or kid, Indira composes a spicier *massalé*–containing also garlic, mustard, ginger, cinnamon, and more cloves–than for a chicken "cari".

More recently, the French on the other side of the Atlantic have started to invent some succulent spice blends often used in their cuisine. The most traditional is the "four spices" that the great Carême was already tossing into his bouillons and simmering saucepans two hundred years ago, when he was cook to the statesman and wit Prince Talleyrand as well as to a long line of kings and emperors.

The French West Indies and the islands of the Indian Ocean offer a vast panoply of recipes rich in flavor and color as well as being strong on temperament. On Martinique and Guadeloupe, spiced dishes called "caris" are flavored with a mix dubbed "Colombo powder" (above) whose attractive color is derived from turmeric. On Réunion, Indian cooks prepare a powdered *massalé* for use in their "curries" or "carries", which owes its brown color to cloves (facing page, with the curry-flavored leaves Roger Vergé uses from his own garden in his spicy recipes). Whatever subtle differences there may be, one problem remains: what wine should one drink with a curry? Wine waiters agree the question is a thorny one but recommend slightly sweet Alsace wines, a *vin jaune* from the Jura, or even certain Brouilly wines.

This blend combines the four sovereigns spices: peppercorns, nutmeg, clove, and ginger, to which Carême also added cinnamon and bay. Without the ginger, but with the cinnamon, one of the greatest of twentieth-century gastronomes, the famous Ali Baba, was to include it—together with the allspice which was meant to impart much the same flavor—in his extraordinary oyster chowder.

The more recent "five berry" mix (sometimes known as "five peppers", but not to be confused with Chinese "five spice powder"), invented around 1980 by the great importer and gourmet Bernard Broquère, includes black, white, and green peppers, "pink peppercorn", and allspice. It can replace ordinary pepper in any recipe, but its fruitiness is best appreciated, fresh from the mill, on salads, mixed grills, omelets or vegetable purées.

The list of these truly great spices can be extended and blended infinitely. New ones brought back by travelers make their appearance, while others resurface from below the distant horizon of the history—and geography—of past gastronomic pleasures. They are to cooking what perfume is to a woman or a smile to a face: one never tires of them. For cooks, they provide that final touch of poetry without which their creations would lack passion and originality. For thousands of years, they have been bringing to our meals, to the very essence of our daily lives, all the pleasure of a magnificent garden, an enchanted garden that sets us on the road to paradise.

The acid pulp of the tamarind (facing page) and the spicy Indian Ocean relish of fruit or vegetables preserved in vinegar known as "achard" (above, right, with lemon in ginger, peppers, and turmeric) are evidence of how spices and condiments can provide a refreshing note of sourness ideal for tropical climes. Nigella ("black cumin", the seed of love-in-a-mist; above, left), meanwhile, gives a peppery warmth when sprinkled onto Indian bread such as *naan*. Spices can fulfill a multiplicity of roles and sharpen the creativity of the food lover. The British were quick to transform ginger into an invigorating jam (next page). Not the least of the many marvels of spices is that they begin by startling the palate—then go on to send it into raptures...

RECIPES

Traditional spice bread

Our present-day Jamaica cakes and other spiced teabreads have their origins perhaps in China, in a honey cake known as "mi kong" which was popular at the courts of the Tang dynasty (tenth century AD). Brought back to Europe by travelers and carefully prepared with a heavy emphasis on cloves and peppercorns in the kitchens of medieval monasteries, by the fifteenth century it had captured the hearts of gourmets from the Balkans and Germany to Champagne and the Rhône Valley. Later on pepper disappeared from the recipe and the quantities of spices were reduced to produce the deliciously melting and spicy teabread that we love today. Certain basic rules need to be followed in order to make a successful spice bread, as perfected by the "guild of spice-bread makers". True spice bread is sweetened only with honey, and its charm depends on the use of authentic spices and aniseed in a combination which manufacturers of mass-produced cake freely admit is impossible to imitate with synthetic flavorings. André Lerch, the celebrated pastry-cook established in Paris since the 1950s, was brought up amid the spice-rich culture of his native Alsace. In the laboratory of his patisserie store, between Boulevard Saint-Germain and the Seine, the warm air rising from his ovens—with quantities of little shortbread biscuits and damson tarts turning golden-brown inside—is laden with the fragrance of cinnamon, cloves and vanilla. He has been kind enough to share with us his family recipe for a truly authentic-tasting spice bread.

Preparation time: 15 min
Cooking time: 45 min

125g (just over 1/2 cup, 4 oz) pure black rye flour
250g (just over 1 cup, 9 oz) Type 55 wheat flour
250g (9 oz) acacia honey
10cl (3 1/2 fl oz, 3/7 cup) milk
8g (1/3 oz) bicarbonate of soda
1 egg yolk
a knob of butter
10g (1/3 oz) pounded aniseed
5g (1/6 oz) cinnamon (powdered)
1 pinch of powdered clove
grated zest of 1 orange
1 pinch of powdered vanilla

(Optional):
candied fruit pieces
grilled split yellow almonds
granulated sugar

Recipe by André Lerch

In a large bowl, mix together the flour, spices, and orange zest. Melt the honey into the milk, add the bicarbonate of soda and fold the flour mix with the egg yolk into the mixture.
This can be oven-baked immediately, but spice bread is better still if the dough is sprinkled with flour and left to stand a few hours—a day is ideal—in a container covered with a cloth, at room temperature.

Pour the mixture into a buttered cake tin and bake for 45 minutes in a preheated oven at 150°C.

After baking, the loaf may be decorated with candied fruit, grilled split almonds, and granulated sugar.

Gazpacho with langoustines and Espelette peppers

Chefs in the French Basque region, taking their inspiration from the incomparably spicy and fruity Espelette pepper, create dishes that are at once simple and subtle, and wonderfully stimulating to the taste buds. An example is this gazpacho with langoustine and Espelette peppers served by Jean-Marie Gautier–winner of the prestigious "Meilleur Ouvrier de France" award in 1991–at the "Rotonde" restaurant in the Hôtel du Palais at Biarritz.

Serves six
Preparation time: 1hr 30 min

30 langoustines
750g (21 oz) ripe red tomatoes
1 sweet red pepper
1/2 green pepper
1 white onion
1/2 cucumber
1 large clove of garlic
3 tbsp sherry vinegar
10cl (3 1/2 oz 3/7 cup) of extra virgin olive oil
1 slice sandwich bread
6 basil leaves
powdered Espelette pepper

Basque recipe by Jean-Marie Gautier

Shell the langoustine tails and set aside in a cool place. Wash all the vegetables and peel the half cucumber.

Dice the green pepper (1/4 inch or so) and put in a cool place.
Chop the tomatoes, cucumber, onion, and red peppers roughly and grind them in a mixer (or on a chopping board); put into a bowl, and add the sherry vinegar.

Peel and finely chop the garlic, add to the gazpacho; salt and season with two pinches of powdered Espelette pepper.

Leave to marinate for one hour in a cool place.

Dice the slice of bread (1/3 inch or so) and fry in olive oil; drain on a kitchen towel and set aside. Fry and salt the prawn tails in hot olive oil, drain on paper towels and sprinkle with powdered Espelette pepper. Serve the gazpacho in soup bowls, garnishing each with five langoustine tails, still warm: sprinkle with diced green pepper and bread, then add the basil leaves.

Rolled pizza from Aleppo

Relatively protected from foreign influences, Syrian food is the very epitome of Middle Eastern cooking today. For gourmets, this is a gastronomic paradise. A few years ago, some exceptional restaurants started opening up in the ancient palaces of the old towns of Damascus and Aleppo, heavy with the scent of the spices from the neighboring souks. These restaurants provide a window onto all the richness of an age-old culinary tradition which is still very much alive among Syrian families.

Evelyne Marty-Marinone lived in Syria for four years, returning home with an array of delicious recipes which she has published in La Cuisine familiale syrienne *(Éditions Publisud). The following Syrian starter which often forms part of a* mezze *is particularly popular in Aleppo, which is one of the major stopping-places–along with Palmyra–along the spice route. This hot rolled "pizza"–tiny and exquisite–is found in little restaurants in the souks. Beahar (or "Aleppo pepper") is a powdered blend of four parts black pepper to one each of cinnamon, cardamom, nutmeg, and clove. This classic mix–close to the old French "four spices"–is sold ready-made in souks, but cooks generally prefer to make their own, modifying the quantities to suit the recipe.*

Serves four
Preparation time : 15 min
Cooking time : 30 min + 2 min

Pizza dough (enough for four small portions)
400g (12 oz) minced lamb
1 tbsp tomato concentrate
1 tsp "Aleppo pepper" mix
1/2 tsp hot pepper paste (harissa or similar)
1 pinch of salt
2 tbsp concentrated pomegranate juice
3 finely chopped onions
1 eggplant
4 small leaves of fresh mint

Syrian recipe

Peel the eggplant and place it in a hot oven (220 C; 400 F) until well cooked (around 30 minutes).

While the eggplant is baking, put the minced meat twice through a meat grinder to make a paste.

Combine all the ingredients (except the mint, eggplant and pizza dough) with the ground meat. Knead well. Shape four pancake circles of dough (roughly the size of a dessert plate) and garnish them with the mixture.

Remove the eggplant from the oven and put the pizzas in for 2 minutes.

Meanwhile, put the eggplant through the mixer.

Decorate the pizzas with a little eggplant mousse and a leaf of mint and roll them up. Serve hot.

Guacamole

A refreshing ode to the pepper, guacamole is a traditional Mexican entrée based on avocados. It is a also a perfect illustration of the Mexicans' thousand-year-old passion for the avocado (a word whose Aztec roots–from ahuacatl–*testify to the fruit's American ancestry) and for hot peppers. Thanks to the vogue for TexMex cuisine, guacamole is today eaten nearly everywhere and can be found ready-made in supermarkets. Nonetheless, few food-lovers have met the genuine guacamole as it is enjoyed in Mexico, which is not just an avocado paste but rather a hearty avocado salad, lightly mashed with a fork and still crunchy.*

This simple and authentic recipe is presented by Michel Javier Drada Ortiz, a chef who has been delighting Paris with his delicious Mexican specialties in his fine food store-cum-restaurant-cum-delicatessen Mexi & Co. There you can also find the ideal pimento for this recipe, the jalapeño, *a small and relatively mild green variety with a good fruity flavor. The* jalapeño *is also sold in American specialty and TexMex-style grocery-stores, in cans or jars. It can be replaced by any other fresh green pimento or by a hot red variety (bird pepper, for example), though in this case a much smaller quantity should be used.*

Serve guacamole with tortilla chips or tostadas *made from ground corn (facing page).*

Serves four
Preparation time : 20 min

10 ripe avocados
juice of 1 lime
3 large ripe tomatoes
1 large sweet onion
5 fresh jalapeño peppers
(or 5 small fresh green pimentos, or
2 whole Cayenne peppers or bird peppers)
2 tbsp oil
2 tbsp vinegar
1 small bunch of fresh coriander
salt

Mexican recipe

Slice the avocados in half, remove the stones and peel the skin; place them cut side down in a dish moistened with the juice of half a lime (to avoid browning).

Rinse the tomatoes and dice them finely. Peel the onion and slice it thinly.

Open the peppers; seed, core, and strip them; slice thinly. Combine the tomatoes, onions, and peppers in a salad bowl with the oil, vinegar, and plenty of salt.

Using the point of a knife, gently notch the flesh of the avocados, squaring them finely and cut them into small pieces.

Mash the avocado pieces gently with a fork, then add the tomato-onion-pepper mixture. Garnish with chopped coriander. (If the dish is not to be served immediately, sprinkle it with the juice of half a lime).

Szechwan beef
with onions and peppercorns

Author of some fifteen books on Chinese cooking, Ken Hom is more than simply a chef: an ever-curious magician, cultivated and much-travelled, he is happy to share his secrets with cooks the world over. Brought up by his Chinese mother in the family restaurant in Chicago's Chinatown, Ken began cooking at the tender age of eleven. The following recipe is a splendid vehicle for the Szechwan pepper that cooks in the West are discovering with increasing relish. The dish is best accompanied by plain white rice. (Cornstarch, soy sauce, and Shaoxing rice wine–China's best-known rice wine–can be found in many Asian grocery stores; sherry may be used instead of rice wine.)

Serves four
Preparation time : 25 min
Cooking time : 10 min

1 lb lean beef steak
3 leeks (white part only, finely shredded)
4 tbsp peanut oil
1 onion, finely sliced
1 tbsp Shaoxing rice wine (or dry sherry)
2 tsp salt
1 tsp sugar
2 tsp sesame oil
2 tsp roasted ground Szechwan peppercorns

Marinade:
1 tbsp light soy sauce
2 tsp sesame oil
1 tbsp Shaoxing rice wine
2 tsp cornstarch

Recipe by Ken Hom

Cut the beef into thin slices 2 in. long and 1/4 in. thick. Put them into a large dish. Add the marinade ingredients and mix well. Leave to marinate for 20 minutes.

Heat a wok or large skillet until very hot. Add the 3 tbsp oil and, when it is very hot and slightly smoking, add the beef slices. Stir-fry for 5 minutes or until lightly browned. Remove and drain well in a colander.

Wipe the wok or pan carefully and reheat it over a high heat until hot. Add the remaining 1 tbsp oil, then add the leeks and onion and stir-fry for 2 minutes.

Add the rice wine and continue to stir-fry for 5-8 minutes. Then add the drained beef slices, salt, sugar, sesame oil, and Szechwan peppercorns, and toss thoroughly to mix.

Turn the mixture onto a serving dish and serve at once.

Fish "cari" with eggplant

Indira Wootun was born and brought up among her Indian family on the Indian Ocean island of Mauritius. Today, she lives in Paris. For over fifteen years, in the restaurant and food store "Aux Spécialités antillaises", she has shared her long experience of West Indian and Mascarenes cuisine, whose distinctive charm lies in its use of spices. Like her mother and her grandmother before her, Indira prefers to prepare her own "Colombo powders", remembering how as a child that she used to crush all the aromatic spices in a mortar. Though today she uses a blender, the result remains the same: a marvelous blend of tastes and smells. For the following delicious West Indian recipe, it is possible to use a ready-mixed ordinary "Colombo powder". But Indira here reveals her secret: a slightly spicier–though far from fiery–version that complements better the stronger flavor of the fish. An intriguing addition to the mix is a few grains of rice to give it that slightly grilled taste.

Serves five
Preparation time: around 1 hr
(plus 2 hrs for the soaking the fish)

5 fillets of fish (sea bream or red snapper)
2 eggplants
5 tomatoes (fresh or peeled and canned)
1 medium onion
1 lime
salt and pepper
1 bunch of fresh coriander
4 or 5 bay leaves
around 50 g (1 1/2 oz) ready-made Colombo
powder (100g (3 oz) per 2.5 kg (5 1/2 lb) of fish)

or better still, Indira's own mixture:
1/4 tsp garlic paste and ginger mixed
1 tbsp ground turmeric
1/2 tbsp cumin
1/2 tbsp coriander seeds
1/4 tsp mustard seed
1/4 tbsp fenugreek
1/4 tbsp cloves
1 pinch cinnamon
1 pinch pepper
1 pinch salt
1/2 tbsp uncooked rice

West Indian recipe

Two hours in advance, steep the fish in the juice of the lime with a little salt and pepper.
If required, prepare Indira's special spice mix: in a skillet, lightly fry all the spices (except the garlic paste, ginger and turmeric) with the rice. Blend the mix. Add the garlic paste and ginger, and ground turmeric. Add a little water to meld into a paste.

Set aside. Fry the fish until golden-brown for 2 to 3 minutes in a large skillet or a high-sided pan in plenty of hot oil. Set aside.

Cut the eggplants into four pieces, salt, and fry in the same oil. Set aside. Leaving only a little oil in the skillet, fry the onion cut into thin rounds.

Once the onion is golden-brown, add the Colombo powder (or the homemade spice paste). Pour in a little water to make a slightly moist paste. Add the bay leaves. Reduce for 1 minute.

Chop the tomatoes into small pieces before adding to the skillet. Simmer gently to obtain a thick sauce.

Add a cup of cold water. As soon as the mixture starts to boil, add the fish fillets, onion and eggplant and simmer again for 10 minutes.

Chop the fresh coriander leaves.

Serve on a large dish sprinkled with coriander; a good accompaniment is pilaf rice.

Risotto "alla milanese"

For centuries, this simple yet delicious risotto with saffron (risotto allo zafferano) has been enjoyed as an everyday dish that brings out all the flavor of this most precious of spices. Today it is often known as risotto alla milanese (Milanese risotto). The art historian Luciana Mottola-Colban–born in Italy but now living in Paris–regales her family and friends with traditional recipes learnt at her mother's knee, dependent on innumerable little secrets and tricks of the trade, and truly successful only when the ingredients are of impeccable quality and flavor. The particular quality of the rice variety is all important, too: the two types of rice that Luciana Mottola-Colban recommends have large, plump grains that are ideally suited to this type of recipe, containing a sort of starch that guarantees a perfectly smooth risotto. These varieties can be found in good Italian foodstores and in the best delicatessens. Finally, if you do not fancy traditional beef marrow, simply leave it out: the result is a rather lighter risotto (which Luciana prefers).

Italian recipe

Prepare the beef stock and remove from the heat.

Crumble the saffron filaments between the fingers or pound them in a mortar (if they are very fresh, warm them for a minute in the oven or in a teaspoon held over a flame to dry them), then let them infuse in half a cup of the hot beef stock.

Chop the beef marrow and the onion very finely, and brown them with a pinch of pepper in 100g (4 oz) of butter over a moderate heat. Meanwhile reheat the stock and simmer on high heat.

When the onion is just beginning to turn golden, turn up the heat, add the rice and keep stirring for one or two minutes (by which time the rice grains should have absorbed the onion-marrow mixture).

When the rice is shiny, moisten it a few times with white wine.

Once the wine has evaporated, reduce the heat. Then, keeping the stock boiling on the other burner, ladle it little by little over the rice until it is cooked. Take care to pour in only a ladleful of stock at a time. For the rice to remain firm, it should never be entirely covered by the stock; it should also not be allowed to evaporate completely between ladlefuls (otherwise the rice will not cook through). Stir the rice carefully throughout cooking.

Once the rice is three-quarters cooked, pour in the saffron infusion. After 17-18 minutes of cooking, remove the risotto from the heat. The rice should be "al dente" (firm) and "all'onda" ("on the crest of the wave", or nicely moist). Add the remaining butter and five generous tbsp of Parmesan, and stir into the rice.
Leave to rest for a few minutes before serving. Serve the rest of the freshly grated Parmesan at the table.

Serves five
Preparation time: 30 min

500g (18 oz, 2 1/4 cups) Carnaroli or Vialone nano rice
150g (6 oz) butter
40g (1 1/2 oz) raw bone marrow
1.5 l (3 pints) beef stock
3/4 glass dry white wine
0.1g (around 40 filaments) saffron
1/2 onion
12 tbsps finely grated Parmesan cheese
a little pepper

Curried eggplant
with *panir* (cottage cheese)

The queen of the spice lands, India is the cradle of one of the world's most sophisticated cuisines. Its subtle flavors derive from precise yet creatively inspired quantities of masalas, *blends of spices that are sometimes known as "curry" mixes. But India also boasts more than one culinary tradition, from the north of the country (and stretching into neighboring Pakistan) influenced by Persia and the Moghul and Muslim conquests—with its chapatis and meat that are oven-cooked in the tandoor—to the very south, based on rice, essentially vegetarian and highly spiced, characterized by the classic hot Madras* masalas, *with coconut milk and tamarind. In the north, the* masalas *are for the most part powders. The great lover of Indian food, amateur cook and businessman Ranjit Rai, who is originally from Lahore and today lives in New Delhi, was encouraged to publish his recipes by his many friends who were dazzled by his cooking. In his books, he acknowledges his debt to his father, who taught him the art of cooking. One of them, Curry, Curry, Curry (Penguin Books India), from which the following recipe is taken, amounts to a veritable ode to the* masala. *A very simple vegetarian dish, this recipe is ideal for lovers of eggplant, here enhanced by a splendid range of spice flavors, "rounded out" by some cottage cheese, the Indian* panir *that can be found in Indian grocery stores (normal cottage cheese or Italian ricotta will do perfectly well instead).*

Serves three or four
Preparation time: 15 min
Cooking time : 40-45 min

2 eggplants
2 medium onions
7 oz (1 cup) cottage cheese (panir)
18 oz tomatoes (to make 5/8 cup tomato puree)
5/8 cup vegetable oil
1/2 tbsp salt (to taste)

spice mix:
1 tsp ginger paste
1 tsp garlic paste
1 tsp turmeric powder
1 tsp coriander powder
1/4 tsp hot chili powder
1/2 tsp caraway powder

Indian recipe by Ranjit Rai

Slice the onions into rings and fry them in oil until golden brown. Set aside on a paper towel. Slice the eggplants (with their skins) into rings of around 1/3 in, sprinkle with a little salt and leave to sweat for 30 mins.

Meanwhile prepare the puree with the peeled tomatoes. Set aside. Wipe the eggplant slices, lightly brown them in hot oil and place them on a paper towel.

Mix the panir (or cottage cheese) well (if it is a touch dry, mash or grate it first) thoroughly with the ingredients of the spice blend. Fry this mixture in the remaining oil for 3-5 mins. (it should be of a creamy consistency).

Transfer into a small baking dish, making alternate layers of eggplant slices and the cottage cheese and spice mix. The topmost layer should be of eggplant.

Pour over the tomato puree and sprinkle lightly with salt.

Cover and bake for 20 min in a moderate oven. Remove the lid and bake for a further 5 min. Before serving, garnish with the fried onion rings.

Velouté of mussels with curry

In this simple recipe combining delicious and mild Cancale Bay mussels with a slightly hot curry mix, Olivier Rœllinger, head chef at the restaurant "Les Maisons de Bricourt", achieves a perfect marriage of very different flavors from two continents, which complement one another without losing their separate identities. First, however, he had to adopt the Indian way, abandoning banal commercial curry powders and blending his own spice mix, which he leaves to mature in a wooden container for at least two weeks: just one of the secrets that this creator of new flavors is happy to share with us. Curry? "But which curry?" he asks in the Livre de Olivier Rœllinger *(Éditions du Rouergue), "There are thousands, from mild to burning hot. In this mix, it is the exact proportion of hot pepper that is crucial, the formula given here being the result of trial and error. Change the proportions to suit your taste, even adding a different spice or two, so as to create your "personal" spice flavor."*

Serves four
Preparation : in three stages, starting two weeks in advance

2 liters of mussels
1 shallot
small glass (7 fl oz) medium dry to sweet white wine (Coteaux du Layon)
single cream
1 tsp curry mix (or more or less, depending on strength)
1 knob of butter
chervil
a few sprigs of blue mint (optional)

Curry spice mix:
20g turmeric powder
22g coriander
10g cumin
10g white pepper
5g cloves
5g cardamom
5g powdered ginger
5g Cayenne pepper
5g mace
5g fennel seed
5g fenugreek
3g star anise

Recipe by Olivier Rœllinger

At least two weeks in advance, prepare the spice mix. Heat together–without water or oil–all the unground spices in a high-sided pan to evaporate the moisture a little; then blend in mixer. To this mixture, add the powdered turmeric and ginger, then leave to mature in a wooden box for at least two weeks before use.

A little over an hour in advance, scrape the mussels clean with a knife, remove the beards, wash thoroughly but do not soak.

Peel and shred the shallot. In a large saucepan (not aluminum), fry the shallots gently in butter. Add the white wine, bring to the boil and tip in the mussels, keeping the mixture covered on a high heat. After 2 minutes, shake the contents of the saucepan; wait a further 2 minutes, check that all the mussels have opened and remove from the heat immediately. (Once open the mussels should cook no further).

Set aside a few whole mussels for the garnish; shell the remainder and set aside.

Strain the cooking liquid. Add the same amount of single cream and quickly bring to the boil. When the sauce begins to thicken, add 1 tsp of the curry mix and leave it to infuse for 5 minutes. At the last minute, bring the sauce gently to a boil, strain, and add the mussels, shelled and whole.

Serve in a soup tureen or in warmed soup bowls, with a little chervil and a perhaps a few leaves of blue mint.

Lamb tajine with prunes

In the fabulously beautiful medinas of Fez, Marrakesh or Meknes, the perfumed spice markets herald Morocco's remarkable culinary tradition, even before you have tasted its cuisine. Boujemaa Mars here presents a truly authentic recipe. An unrivaled master of Moroccan cooking, for twenty years Boujemaa Mars has been head chef at the Hôtel La Mamounia in Marrakesh, a byword for luxury and good living. Tajine means "stew" and is also the name for the earthenware vessel in which these recipes are prepared (facing page, chicken tajine with preserved lemons, diced potatoes and coriander).

Serves four
Preparation and cooking time : 2 hrs

1 kg (2lb 2 oz) lamb (fairly lean and cut into 150g
(5 oz) chunks)
1 bunch of fresh coriander
250g (9 oz, 1 cup) chopped onions
400g (14 oz, 1 3/4 cups) prunes
10 cl (3 1/2 fl oz) olive oil
1g saffron (filaments)
20g (1 oz, 1/8 cup) toasted sesame seeds
10g (1/2 oz) powdered ginger
25g (1 oz, 1/7 cup) chopped garlic
75g (3 oz, 1/2 cup) granulated sugar
1 cinnamon stick
5g (1/5 oz) table salt
5g (1/5 oz) white pepper
100g (4 oz) butter

Moroccan recipe by Boujemaa Mars

Rinse the boned chunks of shoulder and fry them gently with the onions rings, chopped coriander, salt, pepper, ginger, saffron, cinnamon, butter, oil, and chopped garlic.

Cover the meat with water and cook for 1 hour and 30 minutes.

Soak the prunes for 30 minutes in cold water before poaching them in syrup (water and sugar) for 5 minutes.

Arrange the meat on a dish, reduce the sauce and adjust the seasoning to taste.

Top with the prunes, grilled almonds, and sesame seeds.
Serve piping hot.

Produit de France
HEDIARD
Suggestions :
pour parfumer les fruits au sirop,
dans le déglaçage d'un gratin de fruits
de mer ou de langoustes.
VINAIGRE
Vanille de Tahiti
Origine Tahaa
Qualité Extra
FINEST QUALITY
COMPTOIR DES VANILLES
Origine Tahaa
Qualité Extra
FINEST QUALITY

CONNOISSEUR'S GUIDE

THE SPICE BUYER'S GUIDE

SPICE SPECIALISTS

Where can you find good fresh saffron, Szechwan pepper, ras el-hanout or garam masala? Here follows a list of fine grocery stores in the United States, Great Britain, Canada, France and some major European cities offering a wide range of carefully selected spices. This short list is naturally far from exhaustive, for it cannot possibly include all the food stores in the many Chinese, Indian, Arab, Pakistani, Korean, etc. quarters of the world's major cities. When purchasing spices in open-air markets or in loose form, take special care to ensure that they are clean and above all fresh.

UNITED STATES

ADRIANA'S CARAVAN
409 Vanderbilt Street
Brooklyn, NY 11218
(800) 316-0820
(718) 436-8565 in New York
fax (718) 436-8565
e-mail: adriana@aol.com
Cookbook author Adriana Zabarkes offers 1,500 spices, condiments, and other ingredients from around the world. Mail order only.

BALDUCCI'S
424 Sixth Avenue
New York, NY 10011
(800) 225-3822
(212) 673-2600 in New York
Located in New York's Greenwich Village, this bustling food store has a decidedly Italian accent. In person or by mail order, you will find a satisfying selection of spices and herbs among the high-quality gourmet items.

BEZJIAN'S GROCERY
4725 Santa Monica Blvd.
Los Angeles, CA 90029
(213) 663-1503
Middle Eastern spices and foods.

BUENO FOODS
Attn. Mail Order Department
2001 Fourth Street SW
Albuquerque, NM 87102
(800) 95 CHILE

In business for 47 years, this family-owned food company manufactures, prepares, and distributes more than 190 authentic New Mexican food products, including fresh chilies in season. Bueno is one of the nation's largest Hispanic-owned companies.

COYOTE CAFE GENERAL STORE
132 W. Water Street
Santa Fe, NM 87501
(505) 982-2454
Located next to Mark Miller's renowned Coyote Cafe, the General Store offers a variety of chiles, spices, herbs, beans, piñon nuts (pignoli), Mexican chocolate, and other southwestern ingredients.

DEAN & DELUCA
560 Broadway
New York, NY 10012
(800) 221-7714
(212) 431-1691 in New York
www.dean-deluca.com
This popular SoHo food emporium packages its own line of spices and herbs in handsome utilitarian tins that keep out light and air. Entering the store, you will find fresh produce, a bakery, fish and meat counters, and cases filled with cheeses, olives, D&D salads, and other temptations. Packaged foods from around the world, an array of kitchen ware, and shelves of cookbooks round out the selections.

EMERIL SPICES ON-LINE STORE
(800) 545-3024
www.emerilspices.com
Spices, spice blends, and other ingredients used in the renowned New Orleans restaurants of Emeril Lagasse. Also linguica and chourico.

THE GOURMET'S SOURCE
www.gourmetsource.com
fax (802) 483-6250
With 20 years in the food-importing business, this company is the best source for saffron, particularly #1 Mancha. Among the other offerings is Callebaut chocolate.

FRONTIER NATURAL PRODUCTS
P.O. Box 299
Norway, IA 52318
(800) 365-4372
This mail-order company specializes in all-natural food products, including spices, herbs, essential oils, shampoos and lotions, aromatherapy, natural remedies, and vitamins and minerals.

ITALCO FOOD PRODUCTS
1340 S. Cherokee Street
Denver, CO 80223
(303) 722-1882
Spices, oils, vinegars, and more.

SPICE AND GINGER BREADS

Originating in China where it was valued as an aid to digestion, bread baked with spices is today a world-wide tradition. It was introduced into Europe during the fifteenth century. According to the legend, the following recipe was given to Martha Washington by her mother-in-law, and the First Lady served the "gyngerbrede" to Lafayette on his return to America shortly after the Revolutionary War.

1/2 cup vegetable shortening
2 tbsps grated orange zest
1/2 cup packed brown sugar
3 large eggs, well beaten
2 3/4 cups sifted all-purpose flour
1 tsp baking soda
1/2 tsp salt
2 tbsp ground ginger
1 tsp ground cinnamon
1 tsp ground mace
1 tsp ground nutmeg
1 cup molasses
1/2 cup fresh orange juice
1/4 cup brandy

Preheat the oven to 350°F. Grease and flour a 12 x 8 x 2 1/2-inch baking pan. Cream the shortening and orange zest together until fluffy. Add the brown sugar gradually and cream again well. Add the eggs and beat hard for 1 or 2 minutes. Whisk the flour, soda, salt, and spices together and add to the creamed mixture alternately with the molasses, orange juice, and brandy.
Pour the batter into the pan and bake for 30 to 35 minutes, or until the top springs back when pressed.

J & J SPICERY
P.O. Box 1879
Bolingbrook, IL 60440
(630) 378-9335
fax (630) 378-9336
e-mail: spiceryman@aol.com
www.spiceryman.com
Family owned since 1981, this company began by selling at craft fairs and flea markets and now conducts its thriving business on the Internet. Besides the usual, they package their own special blends, Cajun spices, soup and gravy bases, pure extracts, liquid spices, and more. Mail order only.

KALUSTYAN'S
123 Lexington Avenue
New York, NY 10016
(212) 685-3451
In a heady concentration of aromas, the best Asian grocer in Manhattan offers a very good range of fresh spices. Here one can find no fewer than ten different curry pastes. On a shelf of jars and preserves, the choice of preparations is also vast: hot sauces, curry sauces, pepper sauces, saffron cream.

KAM MAN FOOD PRODUCTS
200 Canal Street
New York, NY 10013
(212) 962-8414
A Chinatown landmark, this large emporium sells spices, packaged foods, utensils (this is the best place to get any size wok), dishes, and many other Chinese products.

MACY'S CELLAR
151 W. 34 Street
New York, NY 10001
(212) 695-4400
Located below the ground floor of the "World's Largest Store", the Cellar resembles a village street, with the main aisle in faux brick pavers. On one side of the "street" you will find all the cookware for which Macy's is famous, including the store's own brand. On the other side is an irresistible food hall offering packaged gourmet items and freshly prepared foods of every kind.

PACIFIC GOURMET
P.O. Box 2071
San Rafael, CA 94912
(415) 641-8400
Oils, vinegars, spices, dried mushrooms, olives, chocolate.

SPICES IN PERFUMES

Since early Antiquity, the heady scents of all the major spices have been used to make fine perfumes. Even today, the natural essences of spice enable perfumers to lend an emphatic character to any fragrance. "Bourbon" vanilla gives depth to *Shalimar* by **Guerlain**; cinnamon a hint of ambivalence to **Dior's** *Poison*; cardamom an Eastern personality to *Jungle "L'Éléphant"* by **Kenzo**, to *L'eau d'Hermès*, or to *Elle et Lui* by **Emporio Armani**; cumin a sharp aniseed note to *Mâle* by **Jean-Paul Gaultier**; clove its slightly peppery carnation-like scent to *L'air du temps* by **Nina Ricci** and *Armani pour Homme*; while nutmeg provides a rich palette of aromas for *Cacherel Homme*. The highest accolade should go perhaps to the house of **Gucci**, which in *Envy for Men* has distilled a fragrance that combining ginger, nutmeg, and peppers, among other plant extracts.

PENDERY'S WORLD OF SPICES
304 E. Belknap Street
Fort Worth, TX 76102
(817) 332-3871
Herbs, spices, chilies, and chili powders.

PENZEY'S LTD/
PENZEY'S SPICE HOUSE
P.O. Box 933
Muskego, Wisconsin 53150
(414) 679-7207
Shops also in Brookfield and Madison, Wisconsin; Norwalk, Connecticut; St. Paul, Minnesota.
Impressive and handsome shops with knowledgeable store managers offering advice and tips on storing spices, uses, etc. Penzey's catalog is filled with recipes and info on spices.

PURE AND NATURAL SPICES
4339 Austin Blvd.
Island Park, NY 11558
(516) 889-5116
fax (516) 889-2682
www.pureandnaturalspices.com
Quart-size jars of high-quality spices, herbs, and spice blends are offered at near-wholesale prices; most are $3 (2 for $5) or $4 (2 for $7). Among the large selection are Indian spices, no-salt mixes, and herbal teas and remedies. Customers are billed only the UPS shipping cost, with no handling or packing charge. Mail order only.

RAFAL SPICE COMPANY
2521 Russell Street
Detroit, MI 48207
(800) 228-4276
(313) 259-6373 in Michigan
Large selection of spices and mixes.

SANTA CRUZ CHILI AND SPICE COMPANY
P.O. Box 177
1868 E. Frontage Road
Tumacacori, AZ 85640
(520) 398-2591
Located near the Mexican border, this company manufactures, packages, and distributes its own chile powder, dried chilies, chili paste, and chili flakes, as well as the herbs and spices traditionally used in Mexican cooking. If you are in the neighborhood, stop in at the company store and enjoy the hospitality and the aroma of chilies.

THE SPICE HOUSE
1941 Central Street
Evanston, IL 60201
(847) 328-3711
fax (847) 328-3631;
and
1031 N. Old World Third Street
Milwaukee, WI 53203
(414) 272-0977
fax (414) 272-1271
e-mail: spices@thespicehouse.com
www.thespicehouse.com
With stores in two states, this company has stayed in business for 41 years by building its reputation on quality. Small weekly batch grinding ensures optimum freshness. The spices, herbs, chilies, blends, and seasonings sell at well below grocery store prices, and many are offered in several variations; cinnamon, for example, may be Saigon cassia, China tung hing, Indonesian cassia, Ceylon "true," cassia buds, hard-stick, soft-stick, and so on.

SPICES ETC.
P.O. Box 5266
Charlottesville, VA 22905
(800) 827-6373
fax (800) 827-0145
www.spicesetc.com

Take a look at this lively Web site to find herbs, spices, spice blends, specialty seasonings, dried mushrooms and vegetables, teas, natural flavorings, sauces and mustards, and accessories. You will also find a monthly advice column from "Joe Spice," recipes for blends, and links to other "cool" sites. Mail order only.

STAR MARKET
3349 N. Clark Street
Chicago, IL 60618
(773) 472-0599
Japanese and other Asian ingredients.

WILLIAMS-SONOMA
Mail Order Department
P.O. Box 7456
San Francisco, CA 94120-7456
(800) 541-2233
fax (415) 421-5153
The ultimate source for kitchen tools and furnishings, Williams-Sonoma also offers fine-quality foods, including herbs, spices, sauces, preserves, confections, charcuterie, vinegars, oils, and condiments. Visit one of the elegant stores across the country or shop the catalog to find the perfect spice rack, garlic press, pepper or salt mill, and spice grinder.

ZABAR'S
2245 Broadway (at 80th St.)
New York, NY 10024
(212) 787-2000
An Upper West Side landmark, Zabar's seems to have everything the gourmet cook could desire, including an extensive selection of spices. Enthusiasts travel from all over the city to shop here, so be prepared for crowds on the weekend. The store's upper level is devoted to top-quality kitchen equipment at bargain basement prices.

GREAT BRITAIN

BLUEBIRD GOURMET SHOP
350 Kings Road
London SW3 5UU
Tel : 44 [0]171 559-1000
Terence Conran's marvelous store offers a vast range of spices and strong sauces to transform any menu: a Zulu Fire sauce from South Africa, for example, which, mixed with yoghurt and grated ginger, would make a delicious chicken marinade. Mexican sauces and fruit pickles abound. It is difficult to resist a "necklace" of Rioja peppers strung together–both tasty and ornamental.

FORTNUM & MASON
181 Piccadilly
London W1A 1ER
Tel : 44 [0]171 734-8040
The originality of this famous London firm centres above all on its fine curry mixes, its spicy sauces from many exotic cuisines, and its spiced oils and vinegars. In the cakes section can be found the extraordinary "Grasmere Gingerbread", the recipe for which has remained a closely guarded secret for 130 years.

HARRODS
Knightsbridge
London SW1X 7XL
Tel : 44 [0]171 730-1234
The famous Food Hall offers a choice of pre-packaged spices in jars and above all numerous mixes for Thai, Indian, and Indonesian recipes that tempt you to give the most exotic dinners. A huge range of curry pastes, tandoori, chutneys, and spiced fruits.

JOY
511 Finchley Rd, Hampstead
London NW3 2B
Tel : 44 [0]171 435-7711
Other store: Realfood
14 Clifton Rd, Little Venice, W9.
An excellent shop that can always provide a wide selection of spices (some organic) in packets or loose, together mixes for exotic recipes (ras el-hanout, harissa). At the fresh food counter, fine ginger, galingale, tamarind and even on occasion curry leaves.

LE PONT DE LA TOUR -
OILS & SPICES SHOP
36d Shad Thames
London SE1 2NQ
Tel : 44 [0]171 403-4030
This must be the ideal address: on the very site of the docks at Butler's Wharf where the East India Company used to unload its cargo of spice. This is another fine food grocery store masterminded by Terence Conran, offering a vast selection of spices, some of them rarely encountered.

SELFRIDGES
400 Oxford St
London W1A 1AB
Tel : 44 [0]171 629-1234
In 1999, this architectural monument and shoppers' paradise celebrates its ninetieth year. At the "Culinary World" department in the Food Hall,

SPICE FRAGRANCES IN THE HOME

The scents of spices should not be confined to the kitchen; they can also drift through the rest of the house, thanks to scented candles, home fragrances and *pot-pourris*. **L'Artisan Parfumeur** offers two wonderful deodorizers for the house in their *Terre d'épices* range: *Thé et pain d'épices* and *Île Bourbon*, perfumed with vanilla. These two aromas are available in candles, as a spray or as a diffuser. At the Expo98 in Lisbon, the firm launched *Navegar*, a limited edition scent inspired by the old maritime spice routes, with notes of pepper, star anise, and ginger (also available in candles). The firm of **Diptyque** markets candles perfumed with, among other spices, cinnamon. The specialist in scents for the home, **Jean F. Laporte**, suggests spraying a few drops of *Géranium* or *Bois Précieux* around the house–both scents are brightened with spicy notes–or

else some Gousse, with vanilla and sandalwood, or the peppery *Rose poivrée*. At **Nature et Découvertes**, the *Mémoire d'un instant* range presents candles with a concentrate of fragrance and incense, some with notes of vanilla or cinnamon.

L'Artisan Parfumeur
24 Boulevard Raspail, 75007 Paris
(33) [0]1 42 22 23 32 (and numerous stores in Paris and around France)
Diptyque
24 Boulevard Saint-Germain
75005 Paris (33) [0]1 43 26 45 27
Jean F. Laporte
84bis Rue de Grenelle, 75007 Paris
(33) [0]1 43 44 61 57
Nature et Découvertes
Carrousel du Louvre
(33) [0]1 47 03 47 43
(and numerous stores in Paris and around France)

the fresh spice counter gives off a sublime fragrance. Forty or so spices are on offer, and will be ground for you on demand to the desired quantity.

THE SPICE SHOP
1 Blenheim Crescent
London W11 2EE
Tel : 44 [0]171 221-4448
This attractive shop, situated just opposite the famous food bookshop, "Books for Cooks", offers every spice, splendidly presented. Brigit Erath will be glad to advise you on their use and preparation. Not to be missed when on the hunt for antique bargains in the famous Portobello Market.

FRANCE
Paris

GOUMANYAT & SON ROYAUME
7 Rue de la Michodière
75002 Paris
Tel: 33 [0]1 42 68 09 71
Here excellence meets value for money. Jean-Marie Thiercelin, supplier to some of France's greatest chefs and finest delicatessens, offers every spice (even the rarest) as well as classic mixes, impeccably fresh and of first-rate quality. This heir to a famous saffron supplier founded in 1809 also stocks the very best saffron from La Mancha. All produce is carefully packaged and date-stamped. Also a fine range of oils, vinegars, saffron mustards and other gourmet delicacies.

LA GRAND ÉPICERIE DE PARIS (LE BON MARCHÉ)
38 Rue de Sèvres 75007 Paris
Tel: 33 [0]1 44 39 81 00
A paradise for connoisseurs of top quality spices offering–in addition to the Albert Ménès brand–a wide range of spices, sold by weight, attractively presented and fresh. Spices are sold loose in a little plastic-lined paper sachet. Rarer delights include frosted vanilla pods, as well as gourmet sauces and condiments from the Americas, China, India, and even from Britain (delicious picalilli, for instance). The fresh-food counter has irresistible little chilis.

IZRAËL
30 Rue François-Miron 75004 Paris
Tel: 33 [0]1 42 72 66 23
(see photo pp. 56-57)

SPICES AND CHOCOLATE

Chocolate with peppers was the favorite drink of Aztec nobles and emperors. Spices and cacao complement each other, their flavors harmonizing in the subtlest fashion. The tradition is maintained today by the finest chocolate-makers. First in line is the great **Robert Linxe**, from **La Maison du Chocolat**: his "Flamenco" with basil also contains a barely detectable hint of cardamom and saffron. His "Maiko" is fragrant with a breath of ginger, whereas "Guayaquil" has a whiff of vanilla. Linxe's cinnamon chocolate reaches the pinnacles of gastronomic extravagance. The same is true of that made by **Bernachon**, Lyon's master *chocolatier*, who also sells a plain chocolate tablet with cinnamon and some melt-in-the-mouth truffles flavored with the same spice. **Bernard Dufoux** has created some spice chocolates designed to be eaten as an aperitif, pastilles with cardamom, "Macis" (with mace) and a "Garam Masala". At **Durand**'s, in Rennes, France, the range of spiced chocolates is as wide as it is mouthwatering. Lovers of coffee with cardamom will adore the "Liban", and lovers of cinnamon tea will be seduced by "Canelle". Or be transported to "Vietnam" (with Durand's ginger and lemon grass) or to French Guyana (thanks to "Guyane" with nutmeg, cinnamon and vanilla). While waiting for the boat to Belle-Île, a discovery was made in **Henri Le Roux**, a maker of divine chocolates and caramels in Quiberon. Try his praline with almonds flavored with the old French mix *quatre-epices*, "Vert-Galant"–a slice of stem ginger wrapped in bitter chocolate (the perfect antidote to sea-sickness) or "Szechwan", a *ganache* featuring Szechwan pepper over a nougatine base.

La Maison du Chocolat
225 Faubourg Saint-Honoré
75008 Paris
(33) [0]1 42 27 39 44
Bernachon
42 Cours Franklin Roosevelt
69006 Lyon
(33) [0]4 78 24 37 98
Bernard Dufoux
32 and 40 Rue Centrale
71800 La Clayette
(33) [0]3 85 28 08 10
Durand
5 quai Chateaubriand
35000 Rennes
(33) [0]2 99 78 10 00
Herni le Roux
18 Rue du Port-Maria
56170 Quiberon
(33) [0]2 97 50 06 83

At the best and most captivating grocer's in Paris, it is hardly surprising that the spice counter should be beyond reproach. Every spice imaginable can be found here, usually sold ready-wrapped in little 100g plastic sachets. The roll-call includes hard-to-find spices such as galingale, tonka beans, and sumac, as well as excellent spice mixes prepared by Mrs Solsky. In season, the entire shop is draped with ropes of Espelette peppers. Mr Solsky also stocks Indian spice boxes of every shape and size as well as bamboo graters for fresh ginger.

SHAH & Cie.
33 Rue Notre-Dame-de-Lorette
75009 Paris
Tel: 33 [0]1 42 85 55 16
Though small in size, this is a highly-prized Indian grocer (it is also a fresh food delicatessen). The spices are guaranteed by a quality assurance date on every sachet. Two house specialities are particularly noteworthy: the curry powder mixes, one for meat, the other for fish. The Goulams also provide a mix for tea. The relatively mild Madras mix and the garam masala are also made on the premises. Do not miss their pan masala, the perfect refreshment for the tastebuds after a spicy meal.

SPÉCIALITÉS ANTILLAISES
16 Boulevard de Belleville
75020 Paris
Tel 33 [0]1 43 58 31 30
The most renowned French West Indian restaurant in Paris is also a grocer that sells everything needed for Antillais cooking, as well as for the closely related cuisines of Mauritius and Réunion. The advantage of this store is that the shop assistants are highly qualified cooks who can give you useful and practical tips.

THE SPICES STORE
MBO Services/Spices Store
BP 8338
15 rue des Perdus
95804 Cergy Saint-Christophe
France
fax (33) 1-34-25-44-45
www.spices-store.com
This import-export company specializes in MV brand spices from Jodhpur, India, including some rare items such as black salt and mango powder, plus several curry blends. Shipping to the US begins at $15 per kilogram, but excellent prices make the shipping charge reasonable, and you can order a lot before reaching 1 kilo.

TANG FRÈRES
48 Avenue d'Ivry
75013 Paris
Tel: 33 [0]1 45 70 80 00
Other address: 168 Avenue de Choisy
75013 Paris
The most interesting things in this famous and vast Chinese supermarket are not the countless pre-packaged classic spices (many of the usual French brands are present), but rather the fresh food counter, with its beautiful tamarind, hot peppers, gingers, and sauces and condiments imported from China. The Lee Kum Kee range, for instance, contains essential ingredients for fine Asian cuisine: garlic pastes, Szechwan pepper sauce for hot pepper pastes, mild red pepper sauce, etc. Candied and stem ginger are also available

HANDS-ON COURSES,
MUSEUMS AND ORGANIZATIONS

The best way to learn about cooking with spices is to take a class. To find one in your area, talk to the staff in a gourmet or ethnic shop, or call your community college. For vacation classes and professional training, check **www.shawguides.com** on the Internet. Here are a few outstanding courses, along with museums and organizations where you can learn about spices.

UNITED STATES

AMERICAN SPICE TRADE ASSOCIATION
560 Sylvan Avenue,
P.O. Box 1276,

Englewood Cliffs, NJ 07632
(201) 568-2163
The trade organization ASTA was founded in 1907 and is dedicated to promoting spice consumption and quality. It disseminates a large number of publications on the subject for the lay reader and specialist alike.

ART OF THAI COOKING
P.O. Box 21165
Oakland, CA 94620
(510) 655-8900
e-mail: kasma@lanminds.com
Kasma Loha-unchit offers hands-on classes in Thai, Chinese, and Southeast Asian cooking, as well as food and cultural tours to Thailand. She is the author of *It Rains Fishes: Legends, Traditions and the Joys of Thai Cooking* (Julia Child Award winner).

FRONTERA GRILL/FRONTERA INSTITUTE
445 N. Clark
Chicago, IL 60610
(312) 661-1434
e-mail: rbayl10475@aol.com
Rick Bayless, author of *Authentic Mexican* and *Rick Bayless's Mexican Kitchen* (IACP Cookbook of the Year) offers demonstration classes at his restaurant, Frontera Grill, as well as occasional one-week culinary tours of Oaxaca, Mexico. In 1995 he was recipient of the James Beard Award as Chef of the Year.

JANE BUTEL'S SOUTHWEST COOKING SCHOOL
c/o La Posada de Albuquerque,
125 Second NW
Albuquerque, NM 87102
(800) 472-8229
e-mail cookie@abq.com
www.janebutel.com
Five-day and weekend participation classes which emphasize traditional, innovative, and low-fat southwestern cuisine and include sightseeing and visits to local markets. Butel is the author of 16 cookbooks, including *Jane Butel's Southwest Kitchen and Chili Madness.*

JULIE SAHNI SCHOOL OF INDIAN COOKING
101 Clark Street
Brooklyn Heights, NY 11201
(718) 625-3958
e-mail: jsahni@worldnet.att.net
For 25 years, cookbook author Julie

TEAS FROM THE MISTS OF TIME

The original China tea was made with the addition of ginger. In India, tea has always been flavored with cardamom, cloves, cinnamon (boiling up an infusion of the spice first or simply adding a pinch to the teapot), or with a special tea *masala* with nutmeg, ginger and peppercorns. The best tea purveyors offer many different types of spiced tea. In the United States, the firm of **Bigelow** is renowned for its "Constant Comment" tea, a blend of spices and orange peel, as well as many other spiced black teas, available in many supermarkets. In London, **Fortnum & Mason** offers a wide variety. In France, **Betjeman and Barton** offer the clove-rich *thé aux épices* and the milder "Kipling Tea", containing cinnamon, cardamom and nutmeg (available in the United States through Williams-Sonoma). **Mariage frères** has a vast and bewitching range of teas flavored with a single spice (cinnamon, cardamom, ginger, etc), or of more sophisticated mixes such as "Mandalay", with Burmese cinnamon, Cambodian cardamom, Szechwan peppercorns, and cloves (also available in the United States through Williams-Sonoma). **Les Contes du Thé** offer a tea with cinnamon, cardamom, and clove, as well as a "Thé de Noël" incorporating cinnamon and ginger. The spiciest variety is "Massala" tea, flavored with an elaborate Indian mix.

Le Palais des Thés supplies intriguing cinnamon, cardamom, "Chinese spice" and ginger teas, as well as others flavored with spice mixes.
R.C. Bigelow, Inc.
P.O. Box 880219 - El Paso
TX 88588
Fortnum & Mason
181 Piccadilly - London W1A 1ER
(44) [0]171 734-8040
Betjeman and Barton
23, Boulevard Malesherbes
75008 Paris (33) [0]1 42 65 86 17
Les Contes du Thé
60 Rue du Cherche-Midi
75006 Paris (33) [0]1 45 49 47 60
Mariage frères
30, Rue du Bourg-Tibourg
75004 Paris (33) [0] 42 72 28 11
(two other tearooms/grocers in Paris and outlets outside of Paris)
Les Palais des Thés
35 Rue de l'Abbé-Grégoire
75006 Paris (33) [0]1 45 48 85 81
(five other stores in Paris and outside of Paris)

Sahni (*Classic Indian Cooking, Indian Vegetarian Cooking,* and *Savoring Spices and Herbs*) has taught 3-day hands-on courses in Indian Cooking and Understanding Spices and Herbs. She also offers a 16-day cultural and culinary tour to India.

KAREN LEE IMAGINATIVE COOKING CLASSES
142 West End Ave., 30V
New York, NY 10023
(212) 787-2227
For 25 years cookbook author Karen Lee (*The Occasional Vegetarian, Chinese Cooking Secrets,* and others) has taught hands-on classes in fusion and traditional Chinese cuisine, Italian cuisine, and vegetarian cooking. From September to June, the classes meet in New York's Lincoln Center area, and in July and August, they move to Amagansett, on Long Island.

MOUNT HOREB MUSTARD MUSEUM AND FANCY FOOD EMPORIUM
109 E. Main
Mt. Horeb, WI
(800) 438-6878
(608) 437-3986 in Wisconsin
e-mail: curator@mustardweb.com
www.mustardweb.com
Over 1,500 different mustards in one place, including dill and garlic, lemon herb, hot beer mustard, and Hell in a Jar dried *habañeros.* The award-winning web site includes a catalog, newsletter, recipes, contests, and trivia.

ORIENTAL FOOD MARKET AND COOKING SCHOOL
2801 W. Howard St.,
Chicago, IL 60645
Since 1971 the market has offered demo classes in Thai, Indonesian, Japanese, Korean, Vietnamese, Chinese, and Philippine cooking. Of special interest is an annual 19-day culinary tour of China.

FRANCE

ADAC
85, Rue de Vaugirard
75006 Paris
(from 15h to 18h):
(33) [0]1 42 22 37 41
In the heart of the Paris City Hall's "Ateliers d'expression culturelles et de voisinage", Dominique Bourrellier, food-loving botanist, teaches everything that beginners need to know about spices: botany, history, culture, and their use in various culinary traditions. Courses last a trimester or a full year.

ÉCOLE DES PLANTES
5 Rue Docteur-Roux
75015 Paris
(33) [0]1 40 65 91 84
Botanist Clothilde Boisvert is the vision behind this school offering of courses on botany, with herbal studies and "gastrobotany" for both amateurs and professionals. The scientific study of plants in general–and spices in particular–can be explored here.

MUSÉE DU SAFFRAN
21, Route de Pithiviers
4300 Boynes
(333) [0]2 38 33 13 05

Sixty miles or so from Paris, near the edge of the Beauce and the Gâtinais that was once the heartland of saffron-farming in France, the little town of Boynes established this Museum of Saffron in 1988 in a fine house formerly belonging to a wine-merchant. The ideal place to learn everything about the history of the saffron plantations. At the end of your visit you can even buy a little sample of real Gâtinais saffron, one of the best in the world, of which only a few pounds are produced each year (the Boynes pharmacy also supplies it).

SPICED FRUITS

Fruit and spices have combined to beguile the tastebuds for centuries. For stewed or compote fruits–especially pears, peaches, and cherries–there is nothing like flavoring the cooking water with a pinch of pepper, ground cinnamon, or clove. Some tried and tested combinations: aniseed or star anise with oranges, figs, pineapple, strawberries; cinnamon with oranges, apples, blackcurrants, blackberries, pears, plums, prunes, figs, cherries; cardamom with rhubarb; ginger with pineapple, banana, mango, pawpaw, pears, rhubarb, melon; cloves with pears, peaches, apples, nectarines, oranges, lemons, pawpaw, figs; nutmeg with apples, pawpaw and other exotic fruits; pepper with apples, strawberries, pineapple, figs, melon; vanilla with apricots, peaches, strawberries, pears, apples, figs, pineapple. Spiced fruits can also be purchased in jars ready for use as an accompaniment to duck, pork or game. The French firm Équilibre, a fine food store in Biarritz, offers an interesting range of spiced fruits and vinegars.

RARE VANILLAS

Containing less vanillin but more heliotropin than classic "Bourbon" vanilla, Tahiti vanilla is delicious, expensive and hard to find, though it is available from the French importer **Pacifique Sud**. In the United States, **Williams-Sonoma** offer Nielsen-Massey vanilla, the finest Bourbon vanilla from Madagascar, not only as an extract and as beans but also in powder form. Americans also swear by Mexican vanilla.

Pacifique Sud
Parc d'Activités de Gemenes
800 Avenue du Château de Jonques
13420 Gemenes
(33) [0]4 42 32 02 79
(Fax: 42 32 00 43)

Williams-Sonoma
Mail Order Department
P.O. Box 7456
San Francisco, CA 94120-7456
(800) 541-2233

CHEFS AND THEIR SPICES

Many great cooks are familiar with the secrets of mixing the countless different flavors of spices with skill. For such chefs, spices are a way of bringing out the tastes of foods, and casting fresh light on culinary harmony. These are some of the greatest specialists in spicy cuisine.

Madhur Jaffrey has written award-winning cookbooks that feature the seasonings of her native India as well as other Eastern and Middle Eastern countries. Emphasizing that "spices and seasonings… can transform the same food so it tastes different from day to day," she provides recipes for potatoes cooked with sesame seeds, stewed with soy sauce, or fried with mustard and cumin seeds. Among her books are *A Taste of India* and *Madhur Jaffrey's World-of-the-East Vegetarian Cooking.*

Mark Miller (Coyote Cafe, Santa Fe; Red Sage, Washington DC) is a major contributor to the nation's passion for southwestern and Mexican cooking, opening restaurants and a food store, writing cookbooks, and creating the now-familiar chili posters. He recently teamed up with head chef Mark Kiffen on *Coyote Pantry: Southwestern Seasonings and Home Flavoring Techniques*, in which he divulges the secrets to his authentic natural salsas, flavored oils, dressings, and other sauces and condiments, and gives tips on setting up a southwestern pantry, handling chilies, and using spices.

Mary Sue Millikin and **Susan Feniger** (City Café and Border Grill, Santa Monica, CA) both have training and experience in classic French cooking, but when they became partners in City Café they expanded the menu to feature dishes derived from Mary Sue's travels to Thailand and Susan's explorations of Indian cuisines. On the menu are such well-spiced dishes as Orange Dal with Ginger and Garlic, and Curried Spinach and Eggplant (made with ginger, cumin, ground coriander, ground cardamom, turmeric, ground cloves, and cayenne). After extensive travels in Mexico, the cooking duo launched a second restaurant, Border Grill.

Paul Prudhomme (K-Paul's Louisiana Kitchen, New Orleans) confesses that as a young apprentice chef, he carried his own herb and spice blends in his pocket to toss into the dishes he was preparing. Now his Magic Seasoning Blends are available to all in most supermarkets. His landmark restaurant serves Creole and Cajun dishes using traditional spices and herbs, as well as Prudhomme's latest creations. A generous teacher often seen on television, Prudhomme is also prolific cookbook writer (*Chef Paul's Louisiana Kitchen, Fiery Foods That I Love*, and others).

Wolfgang Puck (Spago and Chinois, Los Angeles) promotes ethnic crossover in his innovative dishes. Inspired by the cuisines of France, Italy, Asia, and the American Southwest, he does not hesitate to combine ingredients from different places. At Chinois, the rack of lamb is French in technique, but the marinade and sauce are decidedly Asian. And the Southwest, Asia, and Italy come together in delightful harmony in the Spicy Chicago Pizza at Spago, which is topped with jalapeño peppers, shiitake mushrooms, cilantro, and fontina and mozzarella cheeses.

Chris Schlesinger (East Coast Grill, Cambridge, MA) has found that spices are an integral part of all hot-weather cuisines. Traveling throughout the tropics–a narrow band along the Equator that he calls the Spice Zone–he has studied local cooking techniques and gathered recipes. In *Big Flavors of the Hot Sun* (co-authored with John Willoughby), he shares his collection of spice rubs and his knowledge of spice lore, along with recipes for Cumin-Crusted Braised Bluefish, Grilled Pompano with Lemon-Cinnamon Sauce, Cardamom Chicken Stew, Apricot-Anise Chutney, and many other tongue-tingling treats.

Rick Tramonto and **Gale Gand** (Brasserie T, Chicago) have modeled their restaurant after the lively, casual eateries of France where hearty food is served with beer. Brasseries originated in Alsace, so the fare has German overtones, and Brasserie T has also embraced Italian and American influences. Unlike haute cuisine, this cooking is robust and highly seasoned. Among the offerings are Spiced Hummus (with cumin, fresh ginger, and cayenne), Fish and Chips in Peppery Amber Beer Batter, Salmon Paillards with Mustard-Dill Sauce, Parmesan-Black Pepper Biscuits (with cayenne and dry mustard), Portofino Bouillabaisse laced with saffron and cayenne, and Ginger Limeade.

SPICED CONSERVES

Spices are not used traditionally in jams–save for the British use of ginger in marmalade. Ginger conserves can be found in stores specializing in fine English foods (Marks and Spencer, for example, and of course Fortnum & Mason). Silver Palate ginger marmalade, meanwhile, retails throughout the United States. In France, **Christine Ferber**, a celebrated conserve-maker from Alsace, uses fresh and natural spices to add zest to fruit jams, including strawberry with black pepper and honey or mint, mirabelles with cinnamon or cardamom, damson or eglantines with vanilla, and quince with "Nostradamus spices" (cinnamon, cardamom, cloves and star anise). Candied fruits and sweet-and-sour condiments include confit of yellow-fleshed peaches with Gerwürztraminer and cloves, and tart wild blackberries with cinnamon, mace, and Pinot Noir.
Maison Ferber
18 Rue des Trois Épis
68230 Niedermorschwihr
(33) [0]3 89270569

Jean-Georges Vongerichten (Vong, JoJo, and Jean Georges, New York City) began his career in his native Alsace, then spent 4 years cooking in Bangkok, Singapore, and Hong Kong. As a result, his culinary style hints of French and Asian influences yet is entirely original. Although intensely flavorful, his recipes use few ingredients and are remarkably simple to make. Among his novel and appealing combinations are Savoy Slaw with Citrus, Ginger and Mustard; Seared Tuna with Szechwan Peppercorns; Salmon in Cardamom Broth; and Broiled Chicken Breast with Cloves.

Georges Blanc (Vonnas) uses no fewer than sixteen spice ingredients as well as garlic in outstandingly subtle "spice weddings". Among these combinations are three more or less hot curry mixes, with mace, Szechwan pepper, hot chili and cinnamon. These are marriages made in heaven, added to a different *plat du jour* each day, be it a frog blanquette, lobster-in-its-shell with tomatos confit and *vin jaune*, or, less elaborately, zucchini *gratin*.

Michel Bras (Laguiole, France) shares with his diners one abiding passion: the taste of sweet-and-spice... At his table, one can enjoy a roast woodpigeon with juniper, oranges and sugar, as well as a number of other marvels in which cane sugar and spices are combined to great effect.

Alain Ducasse (Le Louis XV, Monaco), assisted by Franck Cerutti, produces irresistible delights such as New Spring Lamb from back country Nice, rubbed with Espelette Peppers and Rosemary, roasted in the hearth with Sautéd Offal, or else Pan-fried foie gras of Landes Duck, Celery, Beetroot, fondant Apples and Pears with *dolceforte* Sauce, made syrup of orange juice and honey, basted with duck gravy, with added pepper and spices (coriander, mace, ginger, cinnamon, and black and Szechwan peppercorns).

Phillppe Groult (Amphyclès, Paris) is a true spice lover, composing his own mixes with his customary faultless taste: for his *filet mignon*, he binds six

spices (cumin, paprika, cloves, cardamom, curry powder, Cayenne pepper) with coconut milk. A "Five Spice" mix flavors lobster, while for duck he chooses coriander seeds, bound with honey and draped over the fowl in a most delicious fashion. With summer comes another of his masterpieces, a fruit salad of peaches with white wine, honey and nine spices.

Philippe Jousse (Alain Chapel, Miomay) rightly considers that spices should never be used to disguise the taste of food: from his monkfish with mild garlic there rises the faintest aroma of green anise. The same taste for aniseed is to be found in his crusty baked pear millefeuilles with chocolate and star anise and in a caraway-seed ice-cream.

SAFFRON IN THE GARDEN

Crocus sativus, one of the few spices to thrive in northern Europe, can lend glorious rich purple hues to your garden. Saffron bulbs are available from select nurseries. To ensure flowering, always choose bulbs that have undergone special heat-treatment, purchasing them in August shortly before flowering. The site should be sunny with well-drained soil, if necessary enriched with organic fertilizer.

In the US, bulbs can be mail-ordered from **Van Bourgondien Bros.**, P.O. Box 1000, Babylon, NY 11720 (800) 622-9997; e-mail blooms@dutchbulbs.com or Website: **www.dutchbulbs.com**.

THE COMFORTS OF MULLED WINE

The Greeks flavored their wine with honey and cinnamon and Rabelais sung the praises of "hypocras", a sweet spiced wine perfumed in the Middle Ages with cinnamon and clove. Pepper vodka and Jamaican spiced rum are equally warming. In France, at the Château de La Tuilerie, **Chantal Comte** creates her "Élixir de Carthagène", made from white Grenache with star anise, pink peppercorn, and aniseed, to be drunk *glacé* as an aperitif or as a dessert wine. Another rosé "Carthagène" based on Grenache grapes is flavored with cinnamon, vanilla, nutmeg, and Szechwan peppers, while the scents of cardamom, cinnamon, clove, and Szechwan pepper combine in her "Élixir des Mille et Une Nuits" (of the "Thousand and One Nights") based on red Syrah. "Élixir des Sévillanes", another rosé Grenache,

contains vanilla and nutmeg and is recommended as an aperitif or as a champagne cocktail.
Available by mail order from **Château de La Tuilerie**, Route de Saint-Gilles, 30900 Nîmes. Tel: (33)[0]4 66 70 07 52.

Spiced wine—drunk chilled in summer and mulled in winter—can easily be made at home. This is a simple recipe for either season, as recommended by the major fine food grocer's, Bahadourian of Lyon: in a large saucepan, boil up two glasses of water with six cloves, a cinnamon stick, a little piece of ginger, two tablespoonfuls of sugar, and the zest of two oranges. When a syrup is formed, pour in two bottles of red wine and keep on a high heat without boiling. Serve hot or cold, according to season.

Olivier Rœllinger (Maisons de Bricourt, Cancale, Brittany) presides over his restaurant surrounded by eighty different spices. Among other delights, his "Baby Lobster with Spices" and his "Présalé Saddle of Lamb" (cooked with a dozen spices) are unmissable contemporary classics.

A SHORT GUIDE TO SOME GREAT NAMES

Famous brand leaders in their own country, a few large companies share an ever-expanding market. Here follows a list of the premier brands in the United States and Europe.

Albert Ménès
Founded in 1921, the firm of Albert Ménès has acquired a well-deserved reputation in France. Packaged in high-quality glass vials, the range is today very wide, including some rare spices such as Espelette capiscum and grains of paradise. The company also supplies a large number of spiced biscuits, sauces, and condiments. In France these are available in most supermarkets (see list of addresses for Paris).

Cannamela
Extremely attentive to the quality, cleanliness and proper conservation of their spices, this fine Italian brand offers a very wide selection of products

COCKTAILS WITH A TOUCH OF SPICE

Spices can be used to add piquancy to three classic cocktails: **Alexandra,** made from a milk base, with brandy and cacao, perks up with a small pinch of nutmeg; **Porto flip**–egg yolk, port, brandy and sugar–is also inconceivable without nutmeg; and the ever-popular **Bloody mary**–tomato juice and vodka–was spiced by its creator, the barman at Harry's Bar, Peter Petiot, with a dash of Tabasco. Bernard Merlette, barman at the Hôtel Raphaël in Paris, substitutes little bird-peppers macerated in vodka for the Tabasco.

packaged with care: their little twist-top glass jars, sealed for air-tight freshness, keeps their cinnamon, mace, mild and strong paprikas, peppercorns, and hot peppers in perfect condition. Their "Tappomacina"–jars fitted with mills–are very practical for storing and grinding peppercorns, mace, and hot peppers. Their produce is distributed in many countries.

Ducros
One of the world's leading spice brands, the firm was founded in 1963 by Gilbert Ducros before being sold to the multinational company Montedison. It is Ducros that supplies the majority of French households with spices and herbs thanks to a wide range and clever packaging: their storage jars-come-mills for pepper are wonderful, especially with a five-berry mix inside. Ducros products are sold in supermarkets in France, but also in Spain, Portugal, Italy, Poland and the Middle East.

ISFI
Set up in 1982, the ISFI company has since taken over one third of the Belgian spice market thanks to a policy of consistently high quality. For each spice, the firm insist on only the best producers (a "Muntok" white pepper, for example), selling their products in little glass jars. Apart from Belgium itself, ISFI can be found in supermarkets in Spain, Lebanon, Japan and in the French Territories.

McCormick
McCormick & Company, Inc. is the world's leading spice company. Founded in Baltimore, Maryland, in 1889, it is today present in many countries (known as Schwartz in Great Britain and Club House in Canada). In the

United States, its products are sold under its own name on the East Coast and under that of Schilling on the West Coast. The spices are packaged in small transparent jars and the range is very thorough.

Nordfalks
Well represented in Scandinavia, the Swedish company of Nordfalks, founded in 1946, is famous for its excellent "Santa Maria" brand, especially designed with exotic gastronomy in mind. Numerous spices, but also mixes, sauces, and marinades, give Scandinavians the opportunity of enjoying Indonesian, TexMex, Indian, and Thai receipes in their own homes. Its TexMex products are also distributed in Austria, Spain, Great Britain, Ireland, and the Netherlands.

Ostmann
Founded in 1902, Ostmann is today the largest spice firm in Germany. Through its subsidiaries in South Africa and Great Britain as well as in Austria, it is also established in over thirty other countries. Sold either in little jars or packets, Ostmann offers a very wide range of spices, spiced condiments, and preparations for exotic cooking of exemplary quality.

Schilling (see McCormick)

Schwartz
The result of a merger between the major Canadian spice company, Schwartz, and its British distributor, the mark now belongs to the British offshoot of the American group, McCormick. Market leader in Great Britain, Schwartz supplies a vast range of classic spices (including ten different peppers) and exotic mixes in little

jars or packets. Most interesting are the pastes (ginger, harissa and five spice) that make preparing marinades and sauces easy.

Silvo

King of the spice market in the Netherlands, Van Sillevoldt Specerijen was founded in 1833. Under the trademark "Silvo", it provides a very wide range that is remarkable for its countless blends to be used in exotic cuisine: Indonesian, above all, but also Cajun, TexMex, Indian, Far Eastern, Japanese, Italian, etc. As well as in Holland, the firm is distributed in many European countries: in Britain, its spices can be found in Sainsbury's and Safeway's, at Lidl and Aldi in Germany (and also in the northern and eastern regions of France), and at Ica in Spain.

Spice Islands

Founded in San Francisco in 1941, the American firm Spice Islands offers only spices of high quality prepackaged in glass vials. Their cinnamon (a mixture of the stronger Chinese kind with a sweeter Indonesian variety) and their black peppercorn which is high in piperine from Java (Lampong) are bestsellers in the United States. Spice Islands has become one of the main worldwide producers of spices, herbs, and condiments, and is established in numerous countries.

SPICES ON THE INTERNET

In the United States, there is much talk of spices on the Net. Many spice-importers and sauce, and condiment manufacturers have their own webpage and the theme is a regular one in discussion forums.
Here are just a few sites of interest on the Internet:
www.dean-deluca.com
www.emerilspices.com
www.gourmetsource.com
www.spiceryman.com
www.pureandnaturalspices.com
www.thespicewarehouse.com
www.spicesetc.com
www.spices-store.com
www.shawguides.com
www.janebutel.com
www.mustardweb.com

MILLS AND MORTARS

Mills can cost anything from ten dollars to over a hundred. They can be in natural wood or stained, in see-through or colored plastic, with a handle that turns or one that moves from side-to-side. They can measure from two or three inches high to a foot and a half, be cylindrical, spherical, cubic or ornate–no matter: the only thing that counts when it comes to a pepper mill (which can be used to grind five-berry mix, fenugreek, coriander seeds, etc.) is the quality of its grinding mechanism. Choose grinding wheels in stainless steel, avoiding cast-iron or plastic, which soon wear out. Impeccable mills by **Peugeot**, available throughout the US, offer steel mechanisms with a lifetime guarantee, with a twin row of spiral teeth enabling you to adjust the coarseness of the milling (fine for soups, fillet of fish, omelets, fruits; medium for salads, broiled or roast meats, vegetables; coarse for marinades, steak *au poivre*). **Marlux** offers slightly less expensive mills, including one specially designed for a "mignonette" pepper mix for steak and a clever mill for dried chilis. Both firms also market nutmeg grinders (the nutmeg rotates over a grater). To release all their aromatic depth, cardamom, caraway, cumin, cloves, Szechwan pepper, ginger and chilis should be pounded in a mortar. Mortars can be found in a wide range of materials (granite, marble, earthenware, wood, etc.) and in all sizes: ones with a rough inner surface are especially recommended for fresh spices (ginger and chili). Like Peugeot and Marlux mills, mortars are available from large supermarkets, fine food stores and specialist kitchen suppliers.

A GLOSSARY
OF SPICES

Described here are a number of spices and spice preparations not mentioned in the body of the text. Some are well known to Western palates, but the majority are not common outside the cuisines that traditionally use these spices. You may meet with them during your travels–or else in the most exotic delicatessens–and thus be able to toss something really unexpected into a recipe! (The index lists the pages in the main text at which other spices or spice preparations are described).

Ajowan
Whole or ground, the seeds of this umbel (*Carum ajowan*, also known as *carom*) impart a flavor rather similar to thyme. Ajowan is often used in Indian cookery and is one of the ingredients of certain *masalas*. It is still used in India as a flavoring in paste form for vegetables and fried fish or chicken.

Amchur (mango powder)
In Hindi this word means simply mango powder (under which name it is also sold). In India, the fruit is picked before it ripens, peeled, and cut into thin slices before being sun-dried and powdered. In this form, it is often used to a give a sour flavor to Indian recipes.

Anardhana (see pomegranate)

Asa foetida
As its name implies, asa (or assa) foetida is not blessed with a pleasant smell. The resin of a plant from the genus of the giant fennels, *Ferula assa-foetida*, is used powdered or as a paste in Indian cooking, as an aid to digestion and even for social and religious purposes (certain castes being forbidden to eat garlic, of which its taste is reminiscent).

Curry leaves
Curry leaves come from a plant of Indian origin, *Murraya koenigii*, and are widely employed in Indian cooking thanks to their pronounced curry-like taste. (They should not be confused with the Indian spice mixes (*masalas*)

called "curries" or curry powders" in the West.) The Indians include these leaves in some kinds of green chutney (in which only green-colored ingredients such as mint, green chilies, limes, etc. are used) and, fresh or dried, in spice mixes, often after frying.

Dill
Dill (*Anethum gravoelens*) is popular in Scandinavia. Its fresh leaves give a slightly bitter flavor to smoked or marinated salmon or new potatoes. Dill also flavors famous American dill-pickles, while both the seeds and the fresh plant are frequently used in Indian cooking.

Horseradish
Horseradish is the root of a hardy plant, *Armoracia rusticana*. Grated or passed through the mixer, horseradish is transformed into a hot paste, somewhere between radish and mustard. In the West, horseradish sauce is used to flavor smoked or cured fish such as salmon or herring, or else meat dishes such as roast pork or beef. Very similar is the root of *Wasabi japonica* which gives Japan its *wasabi*, a highly-flavored green-colored cream, the essential adjunct to *sushi* (sliced raw fish).

Ketchup
Ketchup, a sweet condiment of Far Eastern origin made from vegetables, has become universal in its mass-produced tomato-based version. Since its arrival in nineteenth-century England, it has been composed in an ever-growing range of variants. The best are slightly spiced thanks to the addition of hot pepper, ginger, allspice, mace, or black or white pepper.

Mahaleb
Mahaleb is the kernel extracted from the stone of a species of cherry, *Prunus mahaleb*, in Turkey and the Middle East. Powdered, these kernels are used to give a fruity, hazelnut-like flavor to many oriental delicacies (cakes, biscuits, Easter buns among the Armenians, etc.).

Mango powder : see Amchur

Mincemeat
An exquisite mix of candied fruits in brandy (grapes, apples, orange and lemon peels, etc.) and spices (above all nutmeg, but also cloves, cinnamon, mace), mincemeat is an irresistible and very British and American treat, eaten with relish particularly at Christmas when it used to garnish mincemeat pies.

Mustard seeds
Quite apart from the well-known smooth mustard, mustard grains lend their delicious piquancy to other, less everyday preparations. Fried in oil, the

grains of white mustard *(Brassica alba,* cultivated in North America and Europe) give a spicy note to pickles. Seeds of black mustard *(B. nigra* which grows in Asia and in the Middle East) are employed whole or ground as a flavoring in Indian curries. An oil is also made from them and used to flavor fish and vegetables during cooking in northern India. The grains of brown mustard *(B. juncea),* stronger still than yellow mustard, are used in India to spice up yogurts and powdered *masalas,* as well as vegetable dishes.

Pickles

Pickles are vegetables and fruits (onions, carrots, cucumbers, peppers, etc.) soaked in vinegar flavored with a spice mix (including, for instance, dill, allspice, mace, peppercorns, hot or sweet peppers, coriander, ginger, cloves, and cinnamon) which has been previously boiled in vinegar, left to stand and filtered before being added to the vegetables. They are the ideal condiment for pork or other cold meats.

Pomegranate seeds

Dried or made into a juice concentrate, pomegranate seeds impart a delicate acid flavor to the some of best recipes in Middle Eastern and Asian cuisine. In Syria, the concentrate replaces lemons in a number of savory and sweet dishes, imparting a rather sweet and fruity note. In India, the sun-dried seeds (called *anardhana*) are often employed to sour curries. (True French grenadine used to be prepared from pomegranate seeds, but this is unfortunately no longer the case).

Tabasco

Patented in 1870 by its creator, Edmund McIlhenny, Tabasco is by far the most famous hot pepper sauce in the world (140 million bottles sold per year). The peppers (red, or green for the milder version made from Mexican *jalapeños*) are creamed and salted before being fermented in oak casks for three years. Then, after the addition of vinegar, the mixture is packaged in the famous little bottle. In very small quantities, Tabasco may perfectly well be used to give a sour rather than specifically spicy touch to many foods.

Vadouvan

A spice mix (cumin, fenugreek, turmeric, caraway leaves, mustard grains) with fried oil and onions, vadouvan is a fatty Indian preparation added to curried dishes during cooking, to sauces, white meats, rice or potatoes.

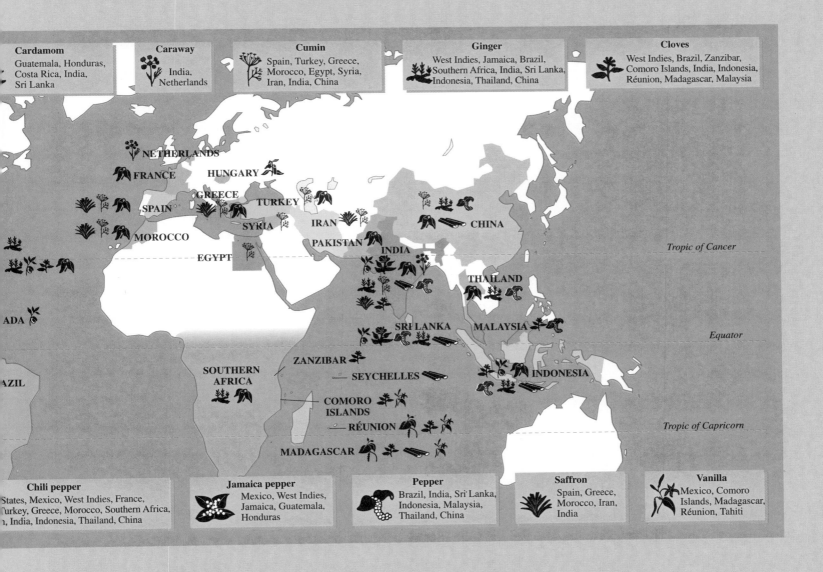

Cardamom
Guatemala, Honduras, Costa Rica, India, Sri Lanka

Caraway
India, Netherlands

Cumin
Spain, Turkey, Greece, Morocco, Egypt, Syria, Iran, India, China

Ginger
West Indies, Jamaica, Brazil, Southern Africa, India, Sri Lanka, Indonesia, Thailand, China

Cloves
West Indies, Brazil, Zanzibar, Comoro Islands, India, Indonesia, Réunion, Madagascar, Malaysia

Chili pepper
States, Mexico, West Indies, France, Turkey, Greece, Morocco, Southern Africa, n, India, Indonesia, Thailand, China

Jamaica pepper
Mexico, West Indies, Jamaica, Guatemala, Honduras

Pepper
Brazil, India, Sri Lanka, Indonesia, Malaysia, Thailand, China

Saffron
Spain, Greece, Morocco, Iran, India

Vanilla
Mexico, Comoro Islands, Madagascar, Réunion, Tahiti

BIBLIOGRAPHIE

General works

American Trade Association. *A Treasury of Spices.* Baltimore: Pridemark Press, 1956.

Bharadwaj, Monisha. *The Indian Spice Kitchen.* New York: E.P. Dutton, 1997.

De la Bedoyere, Charlotte. *How to Grow Culinary Herbs and Spices the Natural Way.* Search Press, 1994.

Garland, Sarah. *The Complete Book of Herbs and Spices: An Illustrated Guide to Growing and Using.* New York: Readers Digest, 1993.

Hayes, Elizabeth S., and J. M. Yeatts. *Spices and Herbs: Lore and Cookery.* New York: Dover Publications, 1983.

Heinerman, John. *Heinerman's Encyclopedia of Healing Herbs and Spices.* Englewood Cliffs, NJ: Prentice-Hall Trade, 1996.

Koch, Maryjo. *Spices: Delectables for All Seasons.* New York: HarperCollins, 1997.

Miloradovich, Milo. *Growing and Using Herbs and Spices.* New York: Dover Publications, 1986.

Norman, Jill. *The Complete Book of Spices.* New York: Viking Studio Books, 1990.

Ortiz, Elisabeth Lambert. *The Encyclopedia of Herbs, Spices, and Flavorings.* New York: Dorling Kindersley, 1994.

Root, Waverley, ed. *Herbs and Spices: A Guide to Culinary Seasoning.* Vanderbilt University, 1985 (reprint).

Simonetti, Walter. *Simon and Schuster's Guide to Herbs and Spices.* New York: Simon & Schuster, 1991.

Skelly, Carole J. *Dictionary of Herbs, Spices, Seasonings, and Natural Flavorings.* New York: Garland Publishing, 1994.

Stuckey, Maggie. *The Complete Spice Book.* New York: St. Martins Press, 1997.

Swahn, J. O. *The Lore of Spices.* New York: Crescent Books, 1995.

Von Welanetz, Diana and Paul. *The Von Welanetz Guide to Ethnic Ingredients.* New York: Warner Books, 1987.

Zabarkes, Adriana and Rochelle. *Adriana's Spice Caravan: Cooking with Spices, Rubs, and Blends from Around the World.* Pownal, VT: Storey Communications, 1997.

History

Apicius, Marcus Garvius. *The Roman Cookery of Apicius.* Trans. and adapted by John Edwards. Emmaus, PA: Rodale Press, 1984.

Corn, Charles. *The Scents of Eden: A Narrative of the Spice Trade.* New York: Kodansha, 1998.

Schivelbusch, Wolfgang, and David Jacobson. *Tastes of Paradise: A Social History of Spices, Stimulants, and Intoxicants.* New York: Vintage Books, 1993.

Tannahill, Reay. *Food in History.* New York: Crown Publishers, 1995.

Toussaint-Samat, Maguelonne. *The History of Food* [1987]. Trans. by Anthea Bell. Cambridge, MA: Blackwell Publishers, 1992.

Cookery

David, Elizabeth. *Spices, Salt and Aromatics in the English Kitchen.* Harmondsworth: Penguin Books, 1970.

Hom, Ken. *Ken Hom's Chinese Kitchen.* Hyperion Books, 1995.

Humphries, John. *The Essential Saffron Companion.* 1996: Grub Street, 1996.

Jaffrey, Madhur. *A Taste of India.* New York: Macmillan, 1998.

Leyel, C.F. *The Gentle Art of Cookery.* London: Chatto & Windus.

Miles, Elizabeth B. *The English silver pocket nutmeg grater.*

Ray, Ranjit. *Tandoor.* Harmondsworth: Penguin Books, 1995.

PHOTOGRAPHIC CREDITS

I N D E X

191

ACKNOWLEDGEMENTS

Alain Stella wishes to express his warmest thanks to all the spice professionals, connoisseurs, and gourmets who have generously given him their help during the writing of this book, kindly offering both their knowledge and their friendly support: Armand Bahadourian, Bernard Brouqère (Le Comptoir Colonial), Mr and Mrs Buchotte (L'Épicier créole), Nathalie Cazaban (Syndicat des producteurs de piment d'Espelette), Michel Javier Drada Ortiz (Mexi & Co.), Lennard Engström (Maison du Danemark), Jean-Marie Gautier (Hôtel du Palais, Biarritz), Ken Hom, Catherine Laroze, André Lerch, Robert Linxe (La Maison du Chocolat), Evelyne Marty-Marinone, Boujemaa Mars (La Mamounia, Marrakech), Bertrand Merlette (Hôtel Raphaël, Paris), Luciana Mottola-Colban, Purnima Rai, Anuradha Ravindranath, Mr Ribeyron-Montmartin (Syndicat National des transformateurs de poivres, épices, aromates et vanille), Nicolas Tisné (Tisné Vanille), Olivier Rœllinger, Jean-Marie Schouvey (Ducros), Gérard Solsky (Izraël), Jean-Marie Thiercelin, Indira Wootun (Aux Spécialités antillaises).

Jacques Boulay would like to extend his thanks to Eric Dubois, the staff at Argile, The Conran Shop, La Compagnie Française de l'Orient et de la Chine, M.A.I. Artisanat indonésien, La Maison de la Vanille, Massis Bleue, N'O and Carrelages Raboni, for their assistance with styling; and, for their valuable aid, Bernadette Boulay, François Cante-Pacos and Jean-Marie Tardy.

The Publishers wish to express their warmest thanks to Olivier Rœllinger who was kind enough to write a preface for this book and who has allowed us to publish one of his delicious recipes. We would also like to thank Jean-Marie Thiercelin, supplier of spices of impeccable quality to the greatest chefs, for having placed at the publisher's disposal a quite exceptional range of spices that have served for all the photographs in close-up printed in this volume (with the exception of the fresh produce, and the ginger and turmeric). Many thanks too to Mrs Thiercelin and to Sandro De Cecco for all the invaluable information they have so patiently provided concerning the colorful and fragrant world of spices.

Thanks are due also to Mr and Mrs Solsky of the firm of Izraël for the materials they have been so kind to lend us and for their patience; also to the Velan Store in Passage Brady and all the stores that have lent us equipment for the photographic illustrations: Bachelier Antiquités, Mariage Frères, La Boutique de Madagascar, Jacques Majewski and Richard Vaché, antique dealers at Châtillon-sur-Seine, La Compagnie Française de l'Orient et de la Chine, The Conran Shop, Liwan, Artisanat indonésien, Pierre Mazorati at the Musée de l'Épicerie d'autrefois, Les Mille Feuilles, N'O, Simrane, Terre d'ailleurs.

The Publishers wishes to express their gratitude to all those who have provided recipes, produce, and advice concerning the use of the spices mentioned: Mr and Mrs Bernanchon (chocolate-makers, Lyon), Chantal Comte (wines, Nîmes), Bernard Dufoux (chocolate-maker, La Clayette), Durand (chocolate-maker, Rennes), Christine Ferber (pastry-cook, Alsace), André Lerch (pastry-cook, Paris), Jean-Marie Gautier (cook, Biarritz), Michel Javier Drada Ortiz (Mexi & Co., Paris), Ken Hom (author), Henri Le Roux (chocolate-maker, Quiberon), Boujemaa Mars (chef, Marrakech), Luciana Mottola-Colban (historian, Paris), Paolo Petrini (chef, Paris), Roger Vergé (chef, Mougins), Indira Wootun (Aux Spécialités antillaises, Paris), not forgetting the publishers who have kindly given their permission to reproduce certain recipes: Anuradha Ravindranath for Ranjit Rai's recipe (p. 172), Danielle Dastugue, Éditions du Rocher, for Olivier Rœllinger's recipe (p. 173) and Éditions Publisud for the recipe by Evelyne Marty-Marinone (p. 165).

Acknowledgement finally to all others who have assisted in the publication of this book: Hélène Bourgois, Bernard Pasquier of the Conservatoire National des Plants à Parfum at Milly-la-Forêt and Danielle de Yparraguire.